Jesus Christ

Self-Denial

or

Self-Esteem?

David M. Tyler, Ph.D.

JESUS CHRIST
Self-Denial or Self-Esteem?

David M. Tyler, Ph.D.

Cover Design by Melanie Schmidt

ISBN: 978-1-936141-26-5

Printed in the United States of America

Focus Publishing
PO Box 665
Bemidji, MN 56619

Then said Jesus unto His disciples,
"If any man will come after me,
let him deny himself,
and take up his cross,
and follow Me."
Matthew 16:24

Contents

Chapter One
Introduction

Some of the most popular themes in psychology are self-image, self-esteem, self-worth, and self-love. The emphasis, regardless of the terminology used by a particular advocate of this movement, is on self.

Over the past twenty-five years the concept of esteeming one's self has had a powerful influence on the church. Before the 1970's the subject of self-esteem was almost unheard of in evangelical circles.[1] Christians, who have generally thought of self-esteem as sinful, have lately been encouraged by beloved Christian authors' books to develop a "healthy" self-esteem. These authors have warned that a negative self-esteem is the basis of most psychological problems and that it even leads to sinful behavior. They have advanced the premise that an individual who does not love himself will find it impossible to develop genuine love relationships with God and others. Self-esteem has been said to be the key that unlocks the door to fulfillment, success, and happiness. It is the proposed answer to nearly all of life's problems.

If the advocates of self-esteem are right, then we must reform our theology. We must change our emphasis from man's unworthiness and focus instead on man's worthiness and his right to esteem himself. The church will need to recognize the tremendous significance that this teaching will have in the lives of individuals, pastors, parents, children, schoolteachers, and so on. Pastors will have a fundamental obligation to their congregations to instruct and nurture them in esteeming themselves. One writer said, "What the church needs more than anything else is a new reformation—nothing else will do! Without a new theological reformation, the Christian church

---

1 Paul Brownback, *The Danger of Self-Love* (Chicago: Moody Press, 1982), p. 12.

as the authentic body of Christ may not survive."[2] The author continued by saying that self-esteem is the universal hope for the church today. In this same vein, James Dobson has said, ". . . the health of an entire society depends on the ease with which its individual members can gain personal acceptance. . . . Personal worth is not something human beings are free to take or leave. We must have it, and when it is unattainable, everybody suffers."[3] Therefore, for the sake of our children, our church, and primarily for ourselves, we must learn to love ourselves. We must not cling to the past. We must change. We must change the way we worship. We must change our parenting methods.

But if the advocates of self-esteem are wrong, then clearly the church's fascination with self-esteem is heretical. Jesus called His followers to imitate Him in denying themselves: "If anyone would come after me, he must deny himself and take up his cross and follow me" (Matthew 16:24). The cross, with all that it symbolizes, permeates and gives meaning and unity to all the ethical teachings of Jesus.[4] Jesus consistently tied together self-denial and the cross. Dietrich Bonhoeffer said, "When Christ calls a man, he bids him come and die. . . . In fact every command of Jesus is a call to die."[5] Bonhoeffer continued by saying that the way of the cross is the path of every Christian. The antithesis of the cross is self-love. Therefore, selfism is classified as a "different gospel" (Galatians 1:6), opposed to the gospel of Jesus Christ.

Because of the extensive appeal and profound acceptance of self-love by evangelicals, a more critical biblical examination of the concept of self-love is needed. Most material on the subject has been written by the proponents of the self-love theory, and little of that has been written from a conservative theological point of view. Fortunately, the tide has begun to turn.

---

2   Robert Schuller, *Self-Esteem: The New Reformation* (Dallas: Word Publishing, 1982), p. 25.

3   James Dobson, *Hide or Seek* (Grand Rapids: Flemming H. Revell, 1971), p. 20, 21.

4   T.B. Maston, *Biblical Ethics* (Cleveland: World Publishing Company, 1967), p. 162.

5   Dietrich Bonhoeffer, *The Cost of Discipleship*, trans. and ed. R.H. Fuller (New York: Macmillan & Company, 1959), p. 79.

There are four impressive books which have provided a critical biblical examination of the concept of self-love. Each provides a general overview of: 1) how the ideas of self-esteem have developed in the secular world and how they passed into evangelicalism and 2) the conflict between selfism and self-denial that is taught in the Scriptures. The first book, *Psychology as Religion: The Cult of Self-Worship*, was written by Paul Vitz. Vitz focuses on the theories of humanistic psychology, which are based on the worship of self. Paul Vitz examines the material from scientific, philosophical, economical, ethical, and religious points of view. In chapter eight, Vitz provides a thoughtful Christian critique of selfism. He points out that the glorification of self is opposed to the Christian injunction to lose self. Vitz says, "Jesus neither lived nor advocated a life that would qualify by today's standards as 'self-actualized.' For the Christian, the self is the problem, not the potential paradise."[6]

The second book, *The Danger of Self-Love*, was written by Paul Brownback. Brownback rightly contends that the greatest book ever written on personality is the Bible. Therefore, he assumes that if self-love were a significant aspect of personality, the Bible would have had a great deal to say about it. The fact is, Brownback continues, the Bible is silent when it comes to the subject of self-love. Brownback discusses the basis of self-love, which is unconditional love based on our humanness, and not on our performance. This idea is found in much of the writings of Christians, as well as secular self-theorists. The Christian approach, however, is based on the argument that an individual can feel good about himself regardless of his performance because God accepts him unconditionally. Brownback points out that there is a great deal of Scriptural evidence that calls these conclusions into question. The final chapters (13-16) of Brownback's book discuss the biblical alternatives to self-love and the benefits of the others-oriented way of living that was modeled by Jesus Christ our Lord.

---

6   Paul Vitz, *Psychology as Religion: The Cult of Self-Worship*, (Grand Rapids: William B. Eerdmans, 1977), p. 91.

The third book, *The Biblical View of Self-Esteem, Self-Love, and Self-Image*, was written by Jay Adams. In this book, Adams expounds some of the principle passages that have been used to "prove" that we are to love ourselves. Matthew 22:36-40, Romans 6, Colossians 3, and James 3:9 are referred to most frequently (our Lord's words in Matthew 22:39 are quoted the most by those who advocate self-esteem teaching). Finally, Adams sets forth for his readers the biblical alternative to self-esteem. He points out that Jesus set forth self-denial rather than self-affirmation as the proper way of pleasing God. Adams writes, "Seldom do we read in self-worth literature about self-denial, the one emphasis on self that does run all through the New Testament." Adams concludes by examining some of the key passages in the New Testament that emphasize self-denial: 2 Timothy 3:2; Matthew 16:24, 25; Luke 14:25-27; John 12:25.

The fourth book, *Prophets of Psychoheresy II*, was written by Martin and Deidre Bobgan. This book critiques Dr. James Dobson's commitment to secular psychology and, specifically, the concept of self-esteem that dominates Dobson's work. Like Adams, Brownback, and Vitz, the Bobgans also cite New Testament passages demonstrating the Bible's teaching of self-denial, not self-love.

In contrast to the above works are books by well-known Christian authors who encourage us to develop "healthy" self-esteem. These books include Norman Vincent Peale's *The Power of Positive Thinking*, Harry Emerson Fosdick's *On Being A Real Person*, Robert Schuller's *Self-Love and Self-Esteem: The New Reformation*, Bruce Narramore's *You're Someone Special*, Josh McDowell's *Building Your Self-Image*, Maurice Wagner's *The Sensation of Being Somebody*, Robert McGee's *Search for Significance*, James Dobson's *Hide and Seek*, and Anthony Hoekema's *The Christian Looks at Himself*. These books advance the premise that to love God and one's neighbor one must first love himself. They assert that the church has too often ignored this side of the "biblical" view of man and, as a result, has played a significant role in undermining the self-esteem of its members.

Therefore, they say that teaching self-acceptance and helping Christians overcome their low self-image should be given priority in the church by pastors.

These vast claims made by Christian self-esteem theorists must be tested by the Scriptures. Are their teachings based on a new exegesis of the Scriptures? If not, where did they originate? The answer to that question is that they originated with secular humanists who studied man, not from the view point of God's Word, but from the subjective observation of self and by self. Their theories were accommodated and incorporated into the teachings of the church. Four of the most influential self-theorists are Alfred Adler (*The Practice and Theory of Individual Psychology*), Erich Fromm (*Man for Himself* and *The Art of Loving*), Abraham Maslow (*Motivation and Personality* and *Toward a Psychology of Being*), and Carl Rogers (*On Becoming a Person*). Their ideas of human personality were popularized by such publications as Eric Berne's *Games People Play* (Transactional Analysis), Thomas Harris's *I'm OK—You're OK* (developed from Berne's theory of Transactional Analysis), and Nathaniel Branden's *The Psychology of Self-Esteem* and *Honoring the Self*.

The main emphasis on self in the Bible is self-denial. Self-denial is very seldom mentioned in the writings of the above self-theorists, either secular or Christian. Although self-denial is a practice which lies at the very heart of Christianity, very little has been written on the subject in our day. Nevertheless, without its exercise there can be no conversion, no holiness of life, and no service to our Master.

Love for self motivates an individual to follow his own agenda, vent his feelings, justify self, and blame someone else or something else. He is self-oriented.[7] However, Jesus taught and modeled self-denial over and against self-love. Jesus' focus was on God and one's neighbor. He placed God's will and the

---

7 To be self-oriented means to focus on self. It is characterized by words and phrases such as self-esteem, self-love, self-worth, self-image, self-confidence, feeling significant, feeling good about yourself, self-concept, self-affirmation, feeling competent, healthy pride, self-acceptance, self-centeredness, valuing yourself, selfism, and selfists.

good of others ahead of His own. Jesus was others-oriented.[8] The love of God is antithetical to self-love. It is a sacrificial love. The dissimilarity between Jesus' focus and that of the self-esteem advocate is obvious. To be self-oriented is to walk in darkness. To be others-oriented is to walk in the light.

The purpose of this book is to examine representative samples of the words and actions of the Lord, in order to demonstrate that Jesus taught and modeled self-denial as opposed to self-love. Whereas Jesus focused on God and neighbor, the self-esteem advocates focus on self. These two views, the others-oriented and the self-oriented, are incompatible with one another. An individual cannot esteem himself and take up his cross at the same time. A man cannot serve two masters, for he will ultimately choose one over the other.

The procedure I used in writing this book was exegetical in nature. I based my study on the presupposition that the Bible is the inerrant Word of God, which is able to make men wise. I contended that the Bible is sufficient to help people who are struggling with life's problems and does not need to be supplemented by so-called "truths" discovered through human investigation and observation. This writer holds to a Christian worldview. The one element of such a world view that distinguishes it from all others is the commitment to a theocentric (God-centered) perspective on all of life and thought. Psychology, which is anthropocentric (man-centered) and humanistic, offers a faulty view of man and depreciates the value of Christ's work on the cross. The Bible is the greatest book ever written on personality and behavior. Human wisdom cannot enhance God's revelation. Just as Christ is utterly divine, so Christians are utterly sufficient in Him (Colossians 2:9-10). Theology and psychology cannot be integrated, and because of

8   To be others-oriented means to focus on God and others. It is characterized by words and phrases such as self-denial, self-sacrifice, love of neighbor, love of God, bearing your cross, following Christ, humility, humiliation, meekness, lowliness, imitating Christ, thinking nothing of yourself, esteeming others, submitting to God and others, God-orientation, crucifying self, and being poor in spirit.

the sufficiency of Christ and His Word, they do not need to be integrated. (See Psalm 19:7-14 for one of the most magnificent statements on the sufficiency of Scripture).

Jesus said, "Whoever follows me will never walk in darkness" (John 8:12). These are the words of Christ, by which we are taught to imitate His life; in doing so, we will walk in the light of truth. Man's heart is deceitful and is the source of all his darkness and ignorance (Jeremiah 17:9). Sometimes men are deceived by other people, but more often they are deceived by themselves. Self-deception, without a doubt, is the most common form of deception and the deadliest. Men do wrong because their hearts lie to them. Jesus also said, "Learn from me" (Matthew 11:29). Here our Lord set forth a vital principle: we must always start with Him. If we start with ourselves, our opinions and theories, we will ultimately go wrong in all of our thinking about truth. Sin has corrupted and darkened the mind and heart of every person. Man cannot think straight. For this reason God has given us supernatural revelation in His Word. Man cannot reason his way to the truth. Much of the trouble in the church today is due to the fact that we are so subjective, so interested in ourselves, so egocentric. Martyn Lloyd-Jones said, "The starting point must always be God. . . . The first answer of the gospel can always, in effect, be put in this way: Forget yourself and contemplate God."[9] So this is of supreme importance to us as we come to consider the whole question of self-esteem and self-love. The starting point must always be Jesus Christ and what He said, taught, and modeled. Historically, this has been the evangelical approach to understanding truth and distinguishing it from error. Unfortunately, we are living in a day which is characterized by, above everything else, the word "confusion." Confusion seems to prevail in the church, especially when it comes to defining evangelicalism.

The main tenet of evangelicalism is the great slogan of the Reformation, sola scriptura. The evangelical starts with the

---

9   D.Martyn Lloyd-Jones, *Fellowship with God* (Wheaton: Crossway Books, 1993), p. 100-101.

Bible. The Bible is the evangelical's authority. Today, the term *evangelical* has become clouded, ambiguous, and broad. It has been said that if a man makes certain statements he is evangelical, or if a denomination makes certain statements, that denomination is evangelical. But the term evangelical is obviously a limiting term. The evangelical is one who is entirely subservient to the Bible. He does not start with any extra-biblical authority, as do the integrationists who trust in man's wisdom and reason. The evangelical distrusts reason, but that does not mean that he is anti-intellectual. The philosopher wants to encompass all truth; he wants to categorize and explain everything. That is why Paul's words in 1 Corinthians are so important for us today:

> Where is the wise man? Scholar? Philosopher? Has not God made foolish the wisdom of the world? We do, however, speak a message of wisdom . . . but not the wisdom of this age or of the rulers of this age, who are coming to nothing. No, we speak of God's secret wisdom . . . (1:18, 2:6-7. More generally, see verses 1:17 through chapter 4 with special emphasis on chapter 2.)

Martyn Lloyd-Jones said that there is a place for reason in our faith: "Reason must never determine *what* we believe. The business of reason is to teach us *how* to believe."[10] In other words, reason is an instrument that teaches us how to think, not what to think. John Calvin said that revelation is not an addition to reason and that one cannot reason properly outside of revelation. The evangelical's focus is on the Scriptures as the sole authority. Therefore, evangelicalism is limited, exclusive, and cannot be defined in broad terms. Sadly, there are many Christian self-theorists who are known as evangelicals, but who do not hold the view that the Bible is the sole authority and is sufficient in all matters of life and godliness. These Christians are teaching a neo-orthodox existential theology. This existential teaching has infiltrated evangelicalism. Historical evangelicalism has always

---

10 D.Martyn Lloyd-Jones, *Knowing the Times* (Carlisle: Banner of Truth, 1989), p. 327.

started with the Scriptures. The integrationists, however, have relied on other sources and have used the Bible only in a token, superficial, or illustrative manner. The Scriptures are rarely used to provide a foundational base on which their theories rest. In fact, they have been used to support humanistic views that are hostile and antagonistic toward the Scriptures. Church history substantiates what the Scriptures teach. In other words, when men have spurned the sufficiency of the Scriptures and trusted human reason, they have gone astray. Study of the past and the biographies of those who have defended the faith against men who have tried to exterminate the truth by adding to it shows that the evangelical witness has always intervened and overruled. The evangelical method, which is the orthodox position, begins with Christ and His Word. Both are vital to knowing whether the self-oriented way of life, with its emphasis on self, self-esteem, self-love, and self-acceptance, is biblical or heretical. When one follows Christ, he will learn that Jesus Christ was others-oriented. His focus was not on Himself but on God and His neighbor. In following the 'wisdom' of the personality theories of Adler, Fromm, Maslow, and Rogers, Christians have undermined the plain teachings and examples of Jesus Christ "in whom are hidden all the treasures of wisdom and knowledge" (Colossians 2:3).

A general analysis of Christ's words, miracles, and parables will reveal the Lord's attitude toward self-love and self-denial. As we examine these two theories on self, it will become apparent that the claims made by Christian self-theorists are incompatible with the teachings of Jesus. Jesus never commanded His followers to love themselves, esteem themselves, accept themselves, believe in themselves, develop a healthy self-image, or nurture feelings of significance and worth. Rather, He commanded them to deny themselves, esteem others, seek God first and the good of their neighbor second. The words and actions of our Lord show that He did not teach and model self-love, but instead condemned it. For example, when the disciples bickered among themselves over who would be greatest or more highly esteemed in the kingdom of heaven, Jesus rebuked them and lovingly instructed them in the principles of humility and selflessness. In the parable of the Pharisee and the Sinner, it was the humble and self-loathing sinner who prayed for mercy and was "justified," not the self-oriented Pharisee. It was the Roman centurion's confession of unworthiness that Christ esteemed. The Lord did not correct the man's unworthy attitude toward himself, but instead He praised him for his great faith and healed his dying servant.

Christ's others-oriented attitude is made plain in His words: "The Son of Man did not come to be served, but to serve, and to give his life as a ransom for many" (Matthew 20:28). The cross, with all that it symbolizes, permeates and gives meaning and unity to all the words and actions of the Lord. Christ's love and self-denial are the two great characteristics of His life and teachings. After Peter's great confession, Jesus revealed more fully to His disciples that He would have to go to Jerusalem and suffer, die, and rise again (Matthew 16:21; Mark 8:34; Luke 9:23). It was then that Jesus said, "If anyone would come after me, he must deny himself and take up his cross and follow me" (Matthew 16:24; Mark 8:31; Luke 9:22). In this case, the denial of self and the taking up of a cross are not two separate things. They are two ways of expressing the same idea. They mean that the self will no longer be the center around which one builds one's life. The will and purpose of God will become dominate in one's life. This requires a radical reorientation of one's attitude and life. Love will be directed toward God and one's neighbor rather than toward one's self.

The subject of self-love is complex. Many fine books have been written about it. My objective in this book is a very limited one. It is to provide a broad picture of Jesus' teachings as they relate to self-denial and self-esteem, rather than give an in-depth exegesis of Christ's words, miracles, and parables.

Chapter Two
The Words of Jesus Christ

Illustrations of Jesus' others-oriented way of life and their incompatibility with the self-oriented way of living are seen in Jesus' words and messages. For example, at the age of twelve Jesus sat at the feet of some of Jerusalem's most learned doctors of Old Testament Law (Luke 2:46-47). Although He must have seen through the shallowness of some of His teachers, and doubtless had deeper insight than any of them, He humbly and submissively sat at their feet, listening to them and asking them questions. He was willing to learn all that He could, for the boy Jesus had a holy anxiety to be "about his father's business." In fact, He was emphatic about doing His father's will, for He said, "I *must* be about my Father's business" (v. 49 KJV, emphasis added). These are the first recorded words that Jesus spoke. Years later, during His public ministry Jesus would say to His disciples, "I *must* work the works of him that sent me" (John 9:4). In the Garden of Gethsemane the Lord prayed, "Not as I will, but as you will" (Matthew 26:39). On the cross He cried, "It is finished!" He had done what His father had sent Him to do. His focus was on the Father's business and not on self.

There are few things in life that are absolutely necessary. As important as they are, even food, water, and clothing are secondary to doing the Father's will. If one "seeks first his kingdom and his righteousness," God will provide the lesser things for the maintenance of life (Matthew 6:33). But the self-theorist is emphatic—love for oneself is a "must." Dobson writes, regarding self-love, "We must have it, and when it is unattainable, everybody suffers."[11] Norman Vincent Peale, in his introduction to Robert Schuller's book *Self-Love*, writes: "Self-love is a vital force in human existence and anyone who lacks love of self can never truly live in harmony with the world and realize his

---

11 James Dobson, *Hide and Seek* (Grand Rapids: Flemming H. Revell, 1974), p. 20-21.

or her dreams and goals or enjoy them after attaining them."[12] Larry Crabb writes in his introduction to Josh McDowell's book *Building Your Self-Image*: "Questions about one's self-image won't go away—and they shouldn't. They are important, especially to the thousands of people who are honest enough to admit that something is missing in their Christian experience."[13] But contrary to the teachings of many of the self-theorists, love for self is not the missing experience in most Christians' lives. The missing experience is the blessing of knowing one has obeyed God's will. This is an obvious contrast to the selfist, whose preoccupation is bolstering and experiencing love for himself.

The incompatibility of Jesus' others-oriented way of life with that of the advocates of self-love is also seen in Jesus' baptism, temptation, cleansing of the temple, and His encounters with Nicodemus and the Samaritan woman. These events took place in what is commonly referred to as the year of Christ's inauguration. In all of these, people are commended to imitate the humility of Christ who laid aside all regard for self and devoted Himself completely to the task God had assigned Him.

Beginning with His baptism by John in the river Jordon, Jesus identified with sinful people. In this, as in other things, "he had to be made like his brothers in every way . . . that he might make atonement for the sins of the people" (Hebrews 2:17). Christ's identification with sinful people involved His surrender of Himself for the accomplishment of the great work of redemption that was ahead. The publicans, harlots, and soldiers whose consciences accused them of sin, submitted to John's baptism, confessed their sin, and professed their desire by repentance and reformation. But the circumstances of Christ's life, including His going to John to be baptized, are not to be understood unless we bear in mind that He acted and suffered as the Second Adam, as the federal head and representative of

12 Robert Schuller and Norman Vincent Peale, *Self-Love* (New York: Jove Books, 1978), p. 5.
13 Josh McDowell and Lawrence Crabb, *Building Your Self-Image* (Wheaton: Tyndale House, 1978), p. 16.

humanity, and as the Son of God. Jesus had no sin of the past to cleanse, but there was a great future to which He dedicated Himself in baptism. Therefore, Jesus humbled Himself to all the religious duties of His day. It was incumbent on Him to "fulfill all righteousness." In His baptism Jesus declared His intention to meet the righteous demands of God by Himself undertaking to pay the debts of men. So the baptism was clearly an act of identification. This dedication implied self-sacrifice in due season. Matthew Henry writes, "As soon as ever Christ began to preach, he preached humility, preached it by example . . . . Christ was designed for the highest honors, yet in his first step he thus abases himself."[14]

Jesus' temptation, like His baptism, was an act of identification with sinful men and, therefore, was others-oriented. It was necessary to the purpose of Christ's coming into the world that He should be tempted. It was necessary that He should learn by His own experiences the bitter trials of temptation so that "he is able to help those who are being tempted" (Hebrews 2:18). Therefore, the temptation of Jesus was necessary to the perfecting of Jesus as the Savior of sinners. Charles Haddon Spurgeon said:

> Jesus was tempted as I am . . . Do not dissociate Jesus from yourself. It is a dark room which you are going through, but Jesus went through it before. It is a sharp fight which you are waging, but Jesus has stood foot to foot with the same enemy.[15]

His temptation was part of His humiliation, part of His suffering, part of His redeeming work. In calm submission before the conflict, Jesus followed the Spirit's leading without resistance, without murmuring, and in steadfast determination to encounter the enemy, who is also the greatest enemy of every Christian.

---

14 Matthew Henry, *Commentary*, Vol. 5 (Old Tappan: Flemming H. Revell, n.d.), p. 27.

15 Charles H. Spurgeon, *The Metropolitan Tabernacle Pulpit*, Vol. 31 (Pasadena: Pilgrim Publications, 1980), p. 261-262.

The cleansing of the temple again demonstrated that Jesus was not self-oriented, but others-oriented (John 2:12-17). His focus was on the glory of God, the purity of His house of worship. Jesus found buyers and sellers in the temple. They were turning a religious duty into a business transaction. True worship was forgotten; only the making of money was remembered. It was His Father's house, and, therefore, He could not bear to see it profaned and God dishonored. At the risk of His own life and safety, He cleansed His Father's house. Christ's zeal was entirely self-sacrificial.

Jesus' Interview with Nicodemus is one of the most important passages in Scripture (John 3:1-21). There can be no doubt that Nicodemus had gone to Jesus under the cover of darkness, in the fear of men. He was afraid of what men would think or say or do if his visit to Jesus was known. Jesus did not send him away, even when he had come under those circumstances. Jesus did not stand on His dignity. He did not say, "Go away and come in the daylight." Jesus was the most accessible of all men. Jesus took Nicodemus and dealt with him gently and lovingly. "A bruised reed he will not break, and a smoldering wick he will not snuff out" (Matthew 12:20). If new Christians are going to grow strong in Christ Jesus, they must be dealt with gently in the beginning. Jesus saw that Nicodemus was perplexed and astonished by the things he had heard; nevertheless, Jesus graciously and patiently guided him using examples and metaphors. The climax of Jesus' conversation with Nicodemus came when He told of the particular plan by which the love of God had provided salvation for sinners (John 3:16). Men who truly love others will give to others. Genuine love can always be measured by its self-denials and sacrifices. There was nothing in man to attract God's love; in fact, there was much to repel God's love. Man's fall was deliberate and willful; it was indifferent and rebellious. Nevertheless, God sent His love upon man. God loved sinners so much that He seemed to love them more than His own Son. He did not spare His only Son in order to spare sinners. The Apostle John has shown us, in the case of

Nicodemus, how our Lord dealt graciously with a self-righteous formalist.

In the encounter with the Samaritan woman, we see the condescension of Christ in dealing with a careless sinner, a carnal-minded woman (John 4:4-42). Jesus took His seat on the well. He was tired and thirsty. "Will you give me a drink?" He asked. Wonder of all wonders, the Maker of all springs, the One Who causes the rain to fall on the land, the Lord of the oceans, yet He had no water to drink and no pitcher to get it with. If He had not been so anxious to win a soul, He might have said nothing and kept to Himself. He was not concerned with Himself, but to do "the will of him who sent me and to finish his work" (4:34). The Samaritan woman, the penitent thief, the Philippian jailor, the publican Zacchaeus, are all examples of Christ's readiness to show mercy and to confer full and immediate pardon. "It is His glory that, like a great physician, He will undertake to cure those who are apparently incurable, and that none are too bad for Him to love and heal."[16]

In each of these instances, we learn that Jesus was others-oriented, as opposed to self-oriented. In obedience to the Father's will in saving men from their sins, Christ offered Himself to be baptized by John. For Jesus there was no confession of personal sin; He was yielding Himself to His Father in perfect, loving resignation. He was led by the Spirit into the wilderness to be tempted by the devil—all for our salvation's sake. He cleansed the temple; for it was His Father's house and should not be defiled. To Nicodemus and the Samaritan woman, He was the lover of souls. From the Lord's example we learn that "A life of self-denial subordinates concern for the things of self to those which serve God's will and which advance His glory, and to the things of our fellow men."[17]

16 J.C. Ryle, *Expository Thoughts on the Gospels*, Vol. 3 (Grand Rapids: Zondervan Publishing House, 1951), p. 208.
17 Guenther H. Haas, *Major Themes in the Ethics of John Calvin* (St. Louis: Covenant Theological Seminary, 1985), p. 47.

Jesus was enjoying great popularity (Matthew 4:23-25; 9:8; Mark 3:7; Luke 5:15-16). As He descended from the mountain where He had appointed the twelve to be His apostles, He was confronted once again by a great crowd. The sight of them must have moved Jesus with pity, for they represented a mass of ignorance, sorrow, and sin. The Savior's omniscient eyes looked upon the people with empathy. He saw the multitudes and their sad condition. His heart was stirred at their plight. No one cared for them. They were like sheep without a shepherd. They came, like multitudes before them, to hear His words. Jesus, intending to do them good, drew near to them to speak. His teaching was meant to bless men and women, for "God did not send his Son into the world to condemn the world, but to save the world through him" (John 3:17). Jesus then gave His now famous Sermon on the Mount (Matthew 5-7).

Beginning with the Beatitudes (5:3-12), Jesus repeatedly used the word "blessed." The Lord said that the person whose life is characterized by the Beatitudes is the only kind of person who is truly "blessed," that is, "happy." Happiness is the great question confronting mankind. To the self-oriented person, feelings of self-love are the key ingredient to happiness. Bruce Narramore writes, "Our attitude toward ourselves, our self-concept or our self-image, is one of the most important things we possess. Our self-concept is the source of our personal happiness or lack of it."[18] One would think that if self-esteem were such an important element to man's happiness, the subject would have found its way into the Beatitudes. Certainly there was never a greater or more appropriate opportunity for Christ to instruct and nurture His followers in the doctrines of self-love than here. In the Beatitudes the Savior gave us eight characteristics of blessed people—facets of the character of Jesus Christ Himself. Jesus was concerned about man's attitude toward himself. These Beatitudes indicate clearly the essential difference between the others-oriented Jesus and the self-oriented person. To help us

---

18 Bruce Narramore, *You're Someone Special* (Grand Rapids: Zondervan Publishing House, 1978), p. 11.

better understand Jesus' words as they relate to our self-image; let's consider together the first five Beatitudes.

"Blessed are the poor in spirit" is the first principle of the Kingdom of God. By nature, man esteems himself; he is haughty, self-assertive, and self-sufficient, a disposition which the world admires. But Jesus said, "That which is highly esteemed among men is an abomination in the sight of God" (Luke 16:15). Jesus was speaking of a poverty of spirit, a lowliness of heart, an absence of self-esteem. This does not mean that a person is weak, timid, or afraid. It is not a matter of suppressing one's true personality. To be "poor in spirit" can be illustrated by David when he said, "Who am I, O sovereign Lord, and what is my family, that you have brought me this far?" (2 Samuel 7:18) or Isaiah who said, "Woe to me! I am ruined! For I am a man of unclean lips . . . my eyes have seen the King, the Lord Almighty" (Isaiah 6:5). When Paul preached in Corinth he went ". . . in weakness and fear, and with much trembling" (1 Corinthians 2:3). We see it in Peter, aggressive and confident in nature, yet he said, "Depart from me, for I am a sinful man, O Lord! (Luke 5:8).

All of these were men of great power and natural abilities. Their essential personalities remained, and yet they were "poor in spirit." Poverty of spirit is a complete absence of pride, self-assurance, and self-reliance. A person who is poor in spirit is conscious that he is nothing in the presence of God. Poverty of spirit acknowledges fault, blameworthiness, shame, and sin. Poverty of spirit looks with a holy contempt upon self. Poverty of spirit is an attitude of the soul wherein a person is emptied of self. He is humbled and lowly in his own eyes. He is insignificant. The man who is "poor in spirit" is a selfless man who mourns. Mourning is joined with selflessness. Jesus said, "Blessed are those who mourn." The self-oriented man loves himself, while the others-oriented man loathes himself. "You will loathe yourself for all the evil you have done" (Ezekiel 20:43). Arthur Pink writes:

> The Christian himself has much to mourn over.
> The sins which he now commits . . . are a daily
> sense of grief to him . . . An ever-deepening
> discovery of the depravity of his nature, the
> plague of his heart, the sea of corruption within,
> ever polluting all that he does . . . .[19]

The others-oriented man cries out, "What a wretched man I am! Who will rescue me from this body of death?" (Romans 7:24). He is not boasting in himself; he is grief-stricken about himself. Like Paul, he says, "I know that nothing good lives in me, that is, in my sinful nature" (Romans 7:18). He does not stop with himself, He also mourns because of the sins of others. He mourns over the state of society. He sees the whole world is in a sorrowful position, not because of an "epidemic of inferiority"[20] and poor self-esteem, but because of sin. That was why our Lord Jesus Christ mourned at the grave of Lazarus and when he saw the city of Jerusalem, which had rejected Him, bringing damnation upon themselves.

Jesus also said, "Blessed are the meek." Meekness is having a true view of self. It is an attitude in one's heart with respect to other people and is characterized by the way it expresses itself in one's conduct toward one's neighbor. In other words, meekness is my attitude toward my sinful self (leading me to mourn) and its outworking in my actions toward others. An example would be Abraham's behavior toward his nephew Lot. Without complaining, Abraham allowed the younger man to assert himself over Abraham, giving Lot first choice of the land. That was meekness. We find another example of this in David. David was anointed king but endured Saul's unjust treatment of him without retaliation. We have seen other examples of meekness in the New Testament in the lives of Stephen and Paul. The supreme example was our Lord Jesus Christ. He said,

---

19 Arthur Pink, *An Exposition of the Sermon on the Mount* (Swengel: Bible Truth Depot, 1950), p. 19.

20 James Dobson, *Hide or Seek* (Grand Rapids: Flemming H. Revell, 1971), p. 17.

"Come unto me, all you who are weary and burdened, and I will give you rest. Take my yoke upon you and learn from me, for I am gentle (meek) and humble in heart . . ." Matthew 11:28, 29). The attitude of meekness can be seen in His whole life. It can be seen in how He reacted to other people's scorn and sarcasm and His attitude toward His enemies. It can be seen in His submissiveness to His Father's will. The apostle Paul described Christlike meekness when he wrote: "Do nothing out of selfish ambition or vain conceit, but in humility consider others better than yourselves. Each of you should look not only to your own interests, but also to the interests of others. Your attitude should be the same as Christ Jesus who . . . made himself nothing, taking the very nature of a servant" (Philippians 2:3-5, 7). That is a description of meekness. Meekness is being others-oriented, as opposed to self-oriented.

The fourth Beatitude is, "Blessed are those who hunger and thirst for righteousness . . . ." This Beatitude follows logically from the previous ones. We have been looking at men's helplessness and poverty of spirit, which leads to a mourning over the sin within them. The act of hungering and thirsting for righteousness is the desire to be free from sin in all its forms and in its every manifestation. It means to be free from sin so that one can be right with God. It means to be free from the power of sin. It means to be holy, because God is holy. It is the desire to show forth the fruit of the Spirit in one's daily life. It is a consciousness of one's need to be like Christ Jesus. In other words, it is a desire to be sanctified. There is nothing so intense and painful as hunger and thirst. There is nothing as intense and painful as hungering and thirsting after righteousness. A godly man has such a passion and craving after righteousness that it can only be likened to hunger. His yearning is to be pardoned from his sins. He has a ravenous appetite for godliness. His desire is to be clothed in the righteousness of Christ. He must rid his heart of all pollution and wickedness or they will break his heart. It is the opposite of hungering and thirsting after self-esteem.

Jesus went on to say, "Blessed are the merciful." What does it mean to be merciful? Mercifulness is a compassionate disposition wherein one takes to heart the miseries of others and is ready on all occasions to be instrumental for their good. Merciful people resemble God who "delights to show mercy" (Micah 7:18). Alexander MacClaren writes:

> Poverty of spirit, sorrow, hunger after righteousness bring deep experiences of God's gentle forbearance and bestowing love, and will make us like Him . . . . Our mercifulness, then, is a reflection from His. His ought to be the measure and pattern of ours in depth, scope, extent of self-sacrifice, and freeness of its gifts.[21]

Christ had earlier called His disciples to be "fishers of men" (Matthew 4:18-22). He commissioned them to fish for the souls of men, but first they had to leave all and follow Him. Christ then told His disciples what He designed them to *be*—the salt of the earth (Matthew 5:13). The Beatitudes describe for us what the Christian *is*; Jesus described how the Christian should manifest this character in his behavior toward others. That we should be the salt of the earth clearly implies that the earth is fallen, sinful, and bad. The cause of this pollution is found in the condition of man's heart. Jesus made that clear when He said, "For out of the heart come evil thoughts, murder, adultery, sexual immorality, theft, false testimony, slander" (Matthew 15:19). Like salt, Christians are preservers, by holy example, by zealous efforts, and by prayer. The hope of the wicked is in the selfless hands of the righteous. Abraham prayed for Sodom, and the Lord answered, "For the sake of ten, I will not destroy it" (Genesis 18:32).

Jesus continued in the Sermon on the Mount, saying, "You are the light of the world" (Matthew 5:14). While the world is always representing itself in terms of light, Jesus always spoke of it in terms of darkness. Jesus said of Himself, "I am the

---

21 Alexander MacClaren, *Garlands of Gladness* (Grand Rapids: William B. Eerdmans, 1945), p. 19.

light of the world" (John 8:12). Not only have believers received light from Him, but they become transmitters of that light to others. Jesus said, "Let your light shine before men that they may see your good deeds and praise your Father in heaven" (Matthew 5:16). Everything must be done for God's sake and glory. Self must be crushed in all its subtlety, that God may be highly exalted. Therefore, Christians share the gospel in order to lead men to glorify God. The world is in a state of darkness and pollution. Just as the Lord Jesus Christ had great compassion for people, so His followers have great sorrow for them and desire that they be saved. Although Christ's disciples have been treated with contempt by the world, they are to be a blessing to the world. The church exists for the sake of the world. The church's task is great, and she must labor not for her own ends, but for the benefit of men. Just as Jesus Christ was not concerned about Himself, so the church is to be others-oriented. Children of God, as citizens of the kingdom of heaven, manifest certain characteristics. The Christian is not someone who lives in isolation from the world. As we have already said, they are to be salt and light.

Next, Jesus laid down an additional principle based on His words: "You have heard that it was said, 'Eye for eye, and tooth for tooth.' But I tell you . . . turn to him the other [cheek] . . . let him have your cloak as well . . . go with him two miles. Give to the one who asks . . . Love your enemies . . . ." (Matthew 5:38-44). In these words, we learn not to do wrong to others, to return nothing of what we have suffered, to offer ourselves to the endurance of evil, to be ready to suffer even more evil than the oppressor desires to inflict, not to hate him of whom we suffer such things, but to love him and do him good. Martyn Lloyd-Jones commented on these verses: "Surely there is but one principle in this teaching, and that is man's attitude toward himself . . . Jesus is concerned the whole time about this question of the 'self'. . . we must become dead to self."[22] No man can put into practice what the Lord said in these verses unless he becomes dead to self. This means he is not concerned about personal "rights of self." It

---

22 D. Martyn Lloyd-Jones, *Studies In The Sermon on the Mount* (Grand Rapids: Zondervan Publishing House, 1959), p. 278 – 279.

is the absence of this tendency of constantly "watching out for self," of having "a sensitivity about self," that is so delicate that the slightest disturbance can upset its equilibrium and devastate the individual. The Lord wants to produce in the believer an *indifference to self*, a spirit and attitude that does not take offense easily, retaliate, defend, or avenge oneself for injury or wrong that is done to us. How does one manifest this selflessness in his behavior? Jesus said to "Pray for those who persecute you" (Matthew 5:44). In other words, do good to those who do evil to you. We see this selfless life so perfectly in the Savior. He did not consider Himself at all, "but made himself nothing" (Philippians 2:7), and commanded His disciples to be thus like-minded (v. 5). This exalted teaching of the Lord concluded with the words, "Be perfect, therefore, as your heavenly Father is perfect" (Matthew 5:48). Thus the morbid condition of self-centeredness and self-sensitivity is a complete denial of Jesus' teachings and life example.

In chapter six of Matthew's Gospel, Jesus continued in the Sermon on the Mount by focusing on living in the presence of and in active submission to God the Father. Throughout the chapter, there is the recurring reference to God the Father and to good works which may be corrupted by self-oriented motives. Jesus warned, "Be careful not to do your acts of righteousness before men, to be seen by them" (Matthew 6:1). The main subjects in Matthew chapter six are prayer and fasting. Once again we see the obvious incompatibility of the self-oriented person and the teachings of Jesus. The danger of praying to be seen by men is not only to be seen by them but also to glorify self. In the final analysis, the only reason for pleasing men is to please oneself. This is where the deceitfulness of sin is so apparent. What appears to be a selfless act, is in reality a selfish act. Martyn Lloyd-Jones writes, "According to our Lord it comes down to this: man by nature desires the praise of man more than the praise of God. In desiring the praise of man, what he is really concerned about is his good opinion of himself."[23] That was

---

23 D. Martyn Lloyd-Jones, *Studies in the Sermon on the Mount* (Grand Rapids: William B. Eerdmans, 1960), p. 14.

why the Scribes and Pharisees were denounced by our Lord as being hypocrites. Their religion was entirely external and self-oriented. Jesus said to the Scribes and Pharisees, "You are the ones who justify yourselves in the eyes of men, but God knows your hearts. What is highly valued among men is detestable in God's sight" (Luke 16:15).

Self-esteem proponents place a high value on self-love. They have told us to "build our self-esteem," that we are "somebody," we are "special" and "significant." Dobson writes, "Isn't it about time that you made friends with yourself?"[24] Jesus never taught men to "make friends with themselves" but to deny themselves. Jesus consistently warned that self is the problem. Robert Schuller writes, "The 'will to self-love' is the deepest of all human desires."[25] In the sense that Schuller means this, he is terribly wrong. In the sense that he does not mean it, he is right. It is true; the deepest desire of fallen man is the will to self-love. But far from being a virtue, which is the sense in which Schuller uses it, self-love is the fruit of a depraved heart. Man's desires are always naturally self-oriented. According to the teaching of Scripture, self-love was responsible for the fall. Satan was subtle enough to know the powerful appeal that self would have on Eve. He said, "God is not being fair. God is trying to deprive you of pleasure and knowledge." Eve agreed. The whole trouble was self and self-assertion. Self-esteem is always in defiance of God. It always means that one puts himself on the throne instead of God.

In Matthew 6:19-34, Jesus continues talking about one's life as he lives it before God in the world. He warned of the temptation of worldliness, which takes two forms. First, there is the positive love one may have for the things of the world—the danger of laying up treasures on earth, hoarding them, living one's life in order to amass them (vv.19-24). Second, there is the anxiety, worry, and care one may experience with respect to the

24 James Dobson, *Dr. Dobson Answers Your Questions* (Wheaton: Tyndale House, 1982), p. 309.

25 Robert Schuller, *Self-Esteem: The New Reformation* (Waco: Word Publishing, 1982), p. 33.

things of the world. Man is always thinking about these things, obsessed with these things, dwelling on them, and worrying about them (vv. 25-34). That is the mind of the natural man; he is self-oriented. His focus in life is always on self, self-gratification, and self-honor, whether materially or emotionally. Men have become disciples of modern "pop-psychology" and have been taught that to be self-oriented is virtuous, that being self-oriented is the way to true health, happiness, and usefulness. Men believe that all of the woes of life are due to the debilitating lack of self-esteem, which manifests itself in feelings of inferiority. But contrary to the popular psychological notion that one's emotional health is dependent upon self-esteem,[26]Jesus taught that anxiety characterizes the self-oriented life. Jesus said, "Do not store up for yourselves treasures on earth . . . . But store up for yourselves treasures in heaven . . . ." (Matthew 6:19-20). In other words, be others-oriented. Focus on God. "Therefore I tell you, do not worry about your life . . . O you of little faith" (Matthew 6:25, 30). The problem is not the lack of self-esteem (self-oriented), but the lack of faith in God (others-oriented). Christians are to concentrate on increasing their faith, or, in other words, perfecting their relationship to God as their heavenly Father. "But seek first his kingdom . . . ." Jesus said (v. 33). Put the kingdom of God first, and then God will provide for one's lesser needs such as food, drink, and clothing. If man wants to seek anything, if he wants to be anxious about anything, then he should be anxious about his relationship to the Lord Jesus Christ. Focusing on God, not on self-esteem, is the cure for worry. Worry always involves a failure to appropriate faith.

"When Christ calls a man," writes Dietrich Bonhoeffer, "he bids him come and die."[27] Dying to self is the cost of true discipleship—a price which neither the scribe nor the other man, described only as a disciple, was willing to pay (Matthew 8:18-22). Perhaps their enthusiasm and sudden impulse to follow

26 James Dobson, *Dr. Dobson Answers Your Questions* (Wheaton: Tyndale House, 1982), p. 301, 307-308.

27 Dietrich Bonhoeffer, *The Cost of Discipleship*, trans, and ed., R.H. Fuller (New York: Macmillan & Company, 1959), p. 79.

Christ were the result of all the excitement over Jesus' teachings and miraculous works (Matthew 8:14-17). It was also obvious that their hasty decision to follow Christ was because they had not "counted the cost" (Luke 14:28). Being accustomed to honor and relative ease, they were not willing to suffer reproach, poverty, and persecution. Jesus was a poor man; unlike foxes that have holes and birds that have nests, Jesus had no home of His own. For our sakes Jesus submitted Himself when He came into the world to the shame and distresses of extreme poverty. Our Lord was poor, very poor. Jesus was others-oriented; with very forcible figures of speech, He told the two self-oriented men that they should stop and count the cost, because there were no worldly honors, riches, or rewards in following Him. The life spent following Christ will be a life of self-denial. As John Calvin writes:

> Let us therefore look upon ourselves as warned,
> in his person, not to boast lightly and at ease,
> that we will be the disciples of Christ, while we
> are taking no thought of the cross . . . . The first
> lesson which he gives us, on entering his school,
> is to deny ourselves, and take up his cross.[28]

We have seen Jesus' others-orientation as He instructed the twelve disciples (Matthew 10:1-39). Their mission was to do good to others by preaching, healing the sick, and raising the dead. He commanded them to "Preach this message: The kingdom of heaven is near" (v. 7) for the purpose of arousing the minds of the nation of Israel to God's coming redemption. They were not to seek great things for themselves, but like their Lord, they were to be lowly. Their ministry was to others and they were told not to worry about themselves; God would provide for them: "Do not take along any gold or silver . . . . take no bag for the journey, or extra tunic, or sandals . . . . Do not worry about what to say or how to say it . . . ." (vv. 9-10, 19). In other words, contrary to the advocates of selfism, they were not to trust or believe in themselves. Norman Vincent Peale writes, "Believe in

---

28 John Calvin, *Calvin's Commentary*, Vol.16 (Grand Rapids: Baker Book House, 1981), p. 388.

yourself! Have faith in your abilities . . . . This book will help you believe in yourself and release your inner powers."[29] But Jesus taught to trust only in God. As Proverbs 28:26 says, "He who trusts in himself is a fool."

Jesus continued by reminding them of God's grace toward them and of their duty to be gracious toward others: "Freely you have received, freely give" (Matthew 10:8). He alerted His disciples to their impending persecution and warned them that their acts of selflessness and kindness would be met with acts of hatred and cruelty (vv. 17, 22, 23). Nevertheless, the Lord encouraged them to "take his cross" and follow Him into a life of self-denial (v. 38). Crossbearing was a commonly used figure of the day; it stood for doing something disagreeable or bearing something painful because it was God's will. There was no talk here of protecting one's self-esteem, which, according to selfists, would surely be crushed by the insensitivity that the disciples were to experience. Success and profit are not the motives for Christian service. Christ's disciples serve for the sake of others, expecting nothing in return. The Christian's motto is "Love for Christ and others." For that reason believers should give their best in sacrifice to God.

Other examples of Jesus' others-oriented way of life and its incompatibility with the self-oriented way of life are seen in what has been referred to as the year of opposition. At this time Christ began to talk specifically and frequently about His cross (Matthew 16:21-25; Mark 8:31- 9:1; Luke 9:22-27). He told of His sufferings and He showed how self-denial and pain were to be the destiny of His followers. Peter rebuked the Lord: "Never, Lord! This shall never happen to you!" But Jesus replied, "Get behind me Satan! You are a stumbling block to me; you do not have in mind the things of God, but the things of men." The contrast was made plain by the words: *"The things of God—the things of men."* The things of God are others-oriented, whereas the things of men are self-oriented. The things of God were revealed

---

29 Norman Vincent Peale, *The Power of Positive Thinking* (New York: Fawcett Crest, 1952), p.13.

in Jesus' words about suffering: He "must" go to Jerusalem with full knowledge that He "must" suffer and "must" be killed. When Jesus said "must," He spoke with authority concerning the divine will of God His Father, whose will He came to do. G. Campbell Morgan, commenting on Peter's words, writes:

> The things of men are revealed in Peter's thoughts, Lord, not that; pity thyself, have mercy upon thyself; that be far from thee; anything but that. The things of God; the method of the cross that merges into the victory of resurrection. The things of men; the method of self-seeking that shuns the cross, and ends in ultimate destruction.[30]

The things of God and the things of men, Morgan rightly says, are . . .

> antagonistic ideals, they are mutually destructive. The things of God are a stumbling block to the man who is minding the things of men . . . . But it is equally true that the things of men are a stumbling block to him who minds the things of God.[31]

In other words, the things of God and the things of men cannot be integrated any more than light can exist with darkness (2 Corinthians 6:14), or a man can serve two masters (Matthew 6:24). Self-denial and self-centeredness are mutually exclusive and are destructive to one another. Man cannot be others-oriented and self-oriented at the same time. In consideration of Peter's comments Jesus restated the terms of His discipleship: "If anyone would come after me, he must deny himself and take up his cross and follow me. For whoever wants to save his life will lose it, but whoever loses his life for me will find it" (Matthew 16:24-25). Author, psychologist, and "pioneer in the field of

---

30 G. Campbell Morgan, *The Sifting of Peter* http://articles.ochristian.com/article14251.shtml

31 G. Campbell Morgan, *The Sifting of Peter*, http://articles.ochristian.com/article14251.shtml

self-esteem," Nathaniel Branden writes, "Respect for the life principle" is the highest standard. Branden continues, "To honor self is to be in love with our own life."[32] But Jesus taught, "The man who loves his life [self] will lose it, while the man who hates his life [self] in this world will keep it" (John 12:25). No man can follow Christ unless he denies himself. Writes Andrew Murray, "There is no other choice for us; we must either deny self or deny Christ... It was self that made the devil. Self was the cause of the fall of man. Self must be utterly denied. Self must be ignored, and its every claim rejected."[33] Self is so deeply rooted in men's hearts that it makes them "stumbling blocks" to others, as well as to themselves. But the self-theorist insists that, far from being a stumbling block, selfism is necessary in order to be an effective witness for Christ, to be able to love and accept others.[34] On the contrary, following Christ is conditioned by self-surrender to Him. It is absolutely necessary to the nature of discipleship.

Further, in Matthew 18 there are two important subjects with which Christ dealt. The first is that of greatness, and the second is that of forgiveness. Both subjects illustrate the principle and necessity of self-denial. The first is the principle of greatness in the kingdom of heaven. As they journeyed to Capernaum, an argument started among the disciples as to which of them would be greatest (Matthew 18:4; Mark 9:33-37; Luke 9:46-48). Jesus called a little child who was playing nearby and sat him among them. Matthew Henry writes, "He sets him in the midst of them; not that they might play with him, but that they might learn from him."[35] A little child is a symbol of innocence and humility. When Christ encouraged His followers to be like a little child, He did not extend this indiscriminately to all areas. True, there is

---

32 Nathaniel Branden, *Honoring the Self* (New York: Bantam Books. 1983), xiv, p. 208.

33 Andrew Murray, *Absolute Surrender* (Springdale: Whitaker House, 1981), p. 59.

34 Diane Garland, Kathryn Chapman, and Jerry Pounds, *Christian Self-Esteem* (Nashville: LifeWay Press, 1991), p. 22.

35 Matthew Henry, *Commentary*, vol. 5 (Old Tappan: Flemming H. Revell, n.d.), p.252.

human nature in children as well as adults; therefore, obviously, the comparison must not be too closely or too exactly carried out, for the Scriptures remind us that, "Folly is bound up in the heart of a child . . . ." (Proverbs 22:15). Having simplicity, being unacquainted with degrees of honor, knowing nothing of the ways of the world, being teachable and submissive, are characteristics of a very young child. His innocent confidence was seen as he came to Jesus as soon as he was called. The child was set in the middle of Christ and His disciples. The child did not know it, but he was pre-eminent. He was not conscious of himself. "The essence of humility is unconsciousness of self."[36]

In stark contrast to the simple, unconscious, unworldly child, who exemplified the others-oriented life-style, were the disciples, who depicted the self-oriented life-style. As Jesus and the disciples made their way toward Capernaum, Jesus spoke of His suffering for others. The disciples, on the other hand, disputed among themselves who would be greatest. There was an enormous incongruity between the selfless attitude of Jesus and the self-centered attitude of His disciples. The disciples had forgotten the cross. To them greatness meant "being served." There was no self-emptying, just self-assertion, which led to their quarrel. Proud men can never rest. But men who are poor and humble in spirit dwell in peace. The man that pursues self-love is quickly tempted and overcome in even trifling things. The principle which Jesus wanted to teach His disciples was that, "Whoever humbles himself like this child is the greatest . . . ." Self-forgetfulness is the perfect pattern, and Jesus is the perfect model. He did not think of Himself at all. He only thought of His Father's glory and of man's good. Man,

> . . . even when well-intentioned, is ever consequential and scheming, ever thinking of himself . . . even when professedly doing good . . . . The great ones in the kingdom, on the other hand, throw themselves with such unreservedness into

---

36 H.D.M. Spenser, ed., *The Pulpit Commentary*, vol. 34 (New York: Funk & Wagnalls, n.d.), p. 224.

the work to which they are called, that they have
neither the time nor inclination to inquire what
place they shall obtain in this world or the next.[37]
They are forgetful of self.

After this, Jesus merged His teaching concerning greatness
with His teaching concerning forgiveness. The context seems to
indicate that the dispute among the disciples as to who should be
the greatest had led to harsh words and division. The Lord used
this occasion to instruct them concerning misunderstandings
and quarrels (Matthew 18:15-17). Unresolved problems hurt
everyone; misunderstandings and offenses must be cleared up as
soon as possible. As Jay Adams explains, "God does not allow
for loose ends; rather He insists that every personal difficulty
that arises must be settled. Whatever comes between Christians
must be removed. Every such difference must be cleared up by
reconciliation."[38] The offended brother is instructed to "go"
to the offender and "show him his fault." He is obliged to take
action to initiate reconciliation. This initiating of reconciliation
would give the offending brother an opportunity for explanation
and would allow for the possibility that the brother was unaware
that he was offensive. Often there is no intent to harm, but
the injury is the result of a sensitive self-love. Of course, the
offender must also go (Mathew 5:21-26). Whether one has done
something to his brother or his brother has done something to
him, he is to go. Jay Adams writes, "Picture two brethren who
have had a quarrel and go off in a huff. When they both cool
down, ideally they ought to meet one another on the way to
each other's house seeking reconciliation."[39] The underlying
purpose of Jesus concerning the sinning brother was expressed in
the words, "You have won your brother over." In either case, the
focus is never on self but always on one's brother. The idea that

---

37 Alexander Bruce, *The Training of the Twelve* (Cincinnati: Jennings & Gra-
    ham, n.d.), pp. 178,179.
38 Jay Adams, *The Christian Counselor's Manual* (Grand Rapids: Zondervan
    Publishing House, 1973), p. 52.
39 *Ibid.*, p. 53.

persons should forgive others because it will do them good and help *them* to "get relief" is a widespread, unbiblical notion that stems logically from a focus on self. However, "Jesus taught us to look away from self, to crucify self, deny self, and be concerned instead about God and others."[40]

Furthermore, there were two incidents in the last months before the crucifixion in which Christ once again taught self-denial as opposed to self-esteem. The first incident was the request by James and John to sit next to Jesus (the one on His right hand and the other on His left) in His kingdom (Matthew 20:26-28). The second incident occurred when Jesus passed Zacchaeus in Jericho.

In the first incident, James and John obviously expected a temporal kingdom consisting of worldly pomp and power. This was surprising, since the Lord had spoken twice before and had just previously spoken a third time of His approaching sufferings and self-denial. He told them, "We are going up to Jerusalem, and the Son of Man will be betrayed to the chief priests . . . they will condemn him to death and turn him over to the Gentiles to be mocked and flogged and crucified . . . ." (Matthew 20:18, 19). Their hearts were so preoccupied with visions of the kingdom, thrones, glory, and honor that they seemed incapable of receiving any truth about the cross. When Jesus spoke of His cross and self-denial, they, like Peter (Matthew 16:22), recoiled in horror from such a prospect. Ugly self (in the form of pride, proud conceit over their own worth, the sinful ambition to covet, to excel others in honor and esteem) was the ruthless taskmaster! As Ronald Wallace points out,

> The self, therefore, constitutes the first and most
> continuous and most baffling problem that every
> Christian has to face. The more zeal we have to
> bring our life under the dominion of God, the
> more inner rebellion and contradiction to
> the will of God will be aroused within us by

---

40 Jay Adams, *From Forgiven to Forgiving* (Amityville: Calvary Press, 1994), p. 92.

concupiscence . . . . Our own hearts are the battlefield where by far the fiercest conflicts with evil are to be waged . . . .[41]

Self-denial is least in man's thoughts, and his sinful nature is abhorred by the very sound of it. Therefore, to follow one's nature is to displease God. The apostle Paul says, "For if you live according to the sinful nature, you will die; but if by the Spirit you put to death [KJV, mortify] the misdeeds [sin] of the flesh, you will live" (Romans 8:13). In Colossians 3:5 Paul writes, "Put to death, therefore, whatever belongs to the earthly nature . . . ." But contrary to Jesus' teachings, self-theorist Nathaniel Branden claims:

> From the time we are children, our parents, our teachers . . . assert that it is easy to be selfish and that it takes courage to practice self-sacrifice. But, as anyone who is engaged in psychotherapy knows, it takes courage to do the opposite . . . . To honor the self is anything but easy . . . . Most people begin practicing self-sacrifice almost from the day they are born.[42]

According to Branden, there is no incongruity between self-denial and human nature; men are innately others-oriented.

The phrase, "Just as the Son of Man did not come to be served, but to serve, and to give his life as a ransom for many" sets forth the Lord's teachings that continued to perplex His disciples. Jesus corrected their mistake by "intimating that His kingdom should be of another nature, and the way to be highest in it was to be humble and low, and mean in opinions of ourselves."[43] The Lord not only taught, but also illustrated His teachings by His life. The years of His public ministry were years

---

41 Ronald Wallace, *Calvin's Doctrine of the Christian Life* (Grand Rapids: William B. Eerdmans, n.d.), pp. 57, 58.

42 Nathaniel Branden, *Honoring the Self* (New York: Bantam Books, 1983), p. 204.

43 Matthew Poole, *Commentary*, vol.3 (Mclean: MacDonald Publications, n.d.), p. 56.

of self-sacrificing toil for the good of others. He made Himself a servant to the sick, diseased, and needy. He was always ready to serve them and continually denied Himself both food and rest. But the self-theorist would disagree wholeheartedly. To him, low self-esteem is the parent of all vices. Jesus said He did not come to be served by others, but to serve others. Our Lord's character is the ideal character. The glory of Christ's life lies in its self-denying service.

In the second of these incidents in which Christ taught self-denial as opposed to self-esteem, "Jesus entered Jericho and was passing through. A man by the name of Zacchaeus . . . " (Luke 19:1-10), a well-known publican, was the object of our Lord's compassion and grace. Many who were present were greatly offended at Jesus' kindness toward Zacchaeus and said, "He is gone to be a guest of a sinner." Christ's sympathies were shown toward all men who sought after His love. He would dine with the Pharisees, if invited; and He would dine with the Publicans. If the person Jesus was associating with was rich, and He was accused of caring too much for money, Jesus did not care. If the person was poor, and He was accused of caring too little about respectability, Jesus did not care. "For the Son of Man came to seek and to save what was lost" (Luke 19:10). Lost— what a pathetic word. What pitiful and mournful pictures the word *lost* brings to mind. Only God can comprehend all the evil, sorrow, wretchedness of life, and degradation of character and death, in the word *lost*. The whole world has become a lost world. Christ came into this lost world to seek and save it. The Son of God, determined to restore the lost world, planned everything in preparation for His own coming. In due time Christ Jesus came. He was born of a woman, lived, suffered, died, arose, and ascended back to heaven. He left behind then great work of redemption—the Gospel of the grace of God.

Our Lord had now entered the last week of His life on earth. After the miracle of raising Lazarus, Jesus' fame spread even more widely. Jesus had spent the night at Bethany. A large number of people who had come to the Passover feast walked to Bethany to see Jesus and Lazarus, who had been raised from the dead. These people formed a great company and marched with Jesus toward Jerusalem. Another crowd, which had come out of Jerusalem, met with those coming from Bethany with Jesus and, after forming one great procession, marched into the city escorting the Lord (Matthew 21:1-11; Mark 11:1-11; Luke 19:28-44). Jesus deliberately presented Himself as King. The multitudes expected Him to be a temporal king. They were anxious that He would restore the kingdom to Israel and set them free. But Christ's kingdom would not be characterized by exhibitions of grandeur and egotism, but rather by spirituality and humility. The King of Kings rode into Jerusalem the poorest of all men—He had "no where to lay his head" (Matthew 8:20). There were no banners or silver trumpets to announce His coming. No dignitaries greeted Him with the keys to the city. Poverty characterized His kingdom; He rode into Jerusalem not on a white stallion, but on a borrowed donkey. Showing that Jesus held the inspired Word in high esteem and was careful to fulfill each letter of it, He did all according to God's word to the prophet Zechariah (9:9). "As he approached Jerusalem and saw the city, he wept over it" (Luke 19:41). Jesus' grief was not for Himself, but for others. He knew, as He beheld the city of Jerusalem, that within a week He would carry a cross outside its gates, where He would die. Anyone in Christ's place, with a horrible death before him, would have naturally been thinking of himself, but Jesus was not. The King of this kingdom was selfless and lived for others. Once in His life the Lord rode in triumph: when He went to Jerusalem to suffer and die. What condescension! The King came to be murdered by the men that He made, and in His death, He redeemed them from wrath.

In His final week of earthly ministry, Jesus directly confronted the scribes and Pharisees. Indeed, in all of Christ's preaching, He was never as severe toward any group of people as He was toward these men whose attitudes and practices were so thoroughly opposed to the spirit of the gospel. They were men of pride, worldliness, and tyranny. Jesus directed His words "to the crowds and to his disciples" in order to rectify their mistaken understanding, and to paint for them a true picture of the scribes and Pharisees (Matthew 23:1-39). Christ, who was a righteous judge, condemned the scribes and Pharisees for their hypocrisy. Eight times the Lord said, "Woe to you." This was an expression of His holy indignation, but it also expressed His holy sorrow. The Lord Jesus grieved for the sinful scribes and Pharisees as He condemned them (see v. 37). His words were very stern, but His words were spoken out of love for them. He cared for their souls. The scribes and Pharisees depicted a self-oriented lifestyle, for Christ said of them, "They do all their deeds to be seen by others" (Matthew 23:5). They did things to be seen by men for the purpose of gaining their admiration, and therefore they were self-oriented. Jesus said the scribes and Pharisees "love the place of honor . . . they love to be greeted in the marketplaces . . . and to have men call them 'Rabbi'" (vv. 6-7). In the final analysis, the only reason for pleasing men is to please oneself. The deceitfulness of sin becomes apparent in acts that appear to be others-oriented, but are in actuality self-oriented. To the contrary, Jesus instructed the people not to seek after distinctions, rank, or supremacy, as the scribes and Pharisees did (vv. 8-10). The people were to cultivate true humility, esteem others, and be servants to all. A Christian must not exalt himself by coveting the praises of men, but must lose himself for Christ's sake. The Christian loses himself in exalting Christ.

The institution of the Lord's Supper was celebrated in connection with the eating of the Passover (Matthew 26:17-30; Mark 14:12-16; Luke 22:7-13). The Passover feast had been instituted to foreshadow what the Lord's Supper was to commemorate—Jesus as the sacrifice for the sins of His people (see 1 Corinthians 5:6-9). The Lord demonstrated His lowliness and selfless attitude while the twelve apostles showed forth the workings of human pride, even in this most solemn of occasions. Jesus had washed their feet, but there was still petty bickering among them over who would be greatest in the kingdom. Jesus was others-oriented and was thinking of their good. The apostles were self-oriented, thinking of what they could gain, but not necessarily the good Christ had for them. Pride is the deadliest of all spiritual enemies. It has been the cause of many evils in the church. Pride influences every person's life, but believers must suppress it if we are going to follow Christ.

As the disciples were thinking of earthly greatness, Jesus announced that He was the true Lamb of God and that all other sacrifices were shadows of Him, *the* Sacrifice. The emblems of the Lord's Supper – the bread and wine – set forth the Savior's death. Christ's dying for men is the great doctrine of the church. If one leaves out the cross and self-denial, then Christianity is a dead religion. As John 15:13 says, "Greater love has no one than this, that he lay down his life for his friends." If there was ever a time when it would have been natural and reasonable for Jesus to focus on Himself, it would have surely been at that time. If the Savior, in facing His greatest trial, would have broken down and wept for Himself, no one would have blamed Him or criticized Him. But the Lord Jesus was so absorbed in doing His Father's will that when they departed the house and headed for the Mount of Olives, He led His disciples in a hymn. Charles Haddon Spurgeon writes:[44]

> Blessed Jesus, how wholly wert thou given up! how perfectly consecrated! so that, whereas other men sing when they are marching to their joys, thou didst sing on the way to death; whereas other men lift up their cheerful voices when honor awaits them, thou hast a brave and holy sonnet on thy lips when shame, and spitting, and death were to be thy portion.

The Lord's Supper is to be observed "often" by the church. It is to be observed in "remembrance" of our Lord's voluntary self-sacrifice for our sins.

---

44 Charles H. Spurgeon, *The Metropolitan Tabernacle Pulpit*, vol. 52 (Pasadena: Pilgrim Publications, 1975), p. 171.

At the close of His ministry, Jesus looked forward to His death, resurrection, and ascension. In preparing His disciples for what was to come, the Lord gave them a "new commandment." He said, "As I have loved you, so you must love one another. By this all men will know that you are my disciples, if you love one another" (John 13:34, 35). Love is the distinguishing mark of Christ's followers. The kind of love that Christ spoke of is contrary to man's old nature; it is "patient, kind, does not envy . . . is not proud . . . is not self-seeking" (1 Corinthians 13:4, 5). It is a disposition which reveals itself in benevolent efforts toward others. It is a love that is motivated by and is modeled on Christ's love for His people. Our Savior was about to carry out a glorious deliverance for His people by His death on the cross. He gave us an example of self-denial, contempt for the self-oriented ways of the world, love for man, and zeal for God. F. F. Bruce writes:

> A brotherhood has been created on the basis of Jesus' work for men, and there is a new relationship within that brotherhood . . . . It was new because the love of Christ's friends for Christ's sake was a new thing in the world. Jesus has set the example. He called on them to follow in His steps.[45]

Their self-sacrificing love was proof of their discipleship: "We know that we have passed from death to life, because we love our brothers" (1 John 3:14). Brotherly love is conditional. Only those who have been born-again, "passed from death to life," can and will love this way. Those who love the brothers are brothers. Brotherly love is contingent upon regeneration, not self-esteem. In his book, *The Sensation Of Being Somebody: Building An Adequate Self-Concept*, Maurice E. Wagner claims that when we feel that we are "somebody" (in other words, have a high self-esteem), we automatically regard others as somebody also . . . we

---

45 F. F. Bruce, ed., *The New International Commentary on the New Testament* (Grand Rapids: William B. Eerdmans, 1971), p. 633.

find ourselves loving others . . . we feel loving."[46] Similarly, Bruce Narramore writes, "There is an intimate connection between our love for ourselves and our love and esteem for God and others."[47] However, if love for others is contingent upon self-love, why did the Lord miss this final opportunity to instruct the disciples on the importance of loving themselves?

The Lord, having eaten the Passover and celebrated the supper with His disciples, went with them to the Mount of Olives and entered the Garden of Gethsemane (Matthew 26:39-46; Mark 14:32-42; Luke 22:40-46). Jesus did not go to the Garden of Gethsemane to hide out from His enemies, but to present Himself to His enemies. Jesus had gone to Gethsemane in full knowledge of His coming Passion because He delighted to do the will of the Lord, even though it involved obedience unto death. Jesus experienced that awful and mysterious agony of soul which our words cannot explain and our bodies cannot experience. Jesus told His disciples to remain at a distance, even the three closest ones, for this inner chamber of grief was closed to everyone. John describes Him as saying, "Now my heart is troubled" (12:27). Matthew writes that His "soul is overwhelmed with sorrow" (26:38). Mark records that "He began to be deeply distressed and troubled . . . overwhelmed with sorrow to the point of death" (14:33-34). Luke records Him as "being in anguish . . . and his sweat was like drops of blood falling to the ground" (22:44). Spurgeon writes:

> How black I am, how filthy, how loathsome
> in the sight of God, I feel myself only fit to be
> cast into the lowest hell, and I wonder that
> God has not long ago cast me there; but I go
> to Gethsemane, and I peer under those gnarled
> olive trees, and I see my Savior. Yes, I see him
> wallowing on the ground in anguish and hear

---

46 Maurice Wagner, *The Sensation of Being Somebody: Building an Adequate Self-Concept* (Grand Rapids: Zondervan Publishing House, 1975), p. 175.

47 Bruce Narramore, *You're Someone Special* (Grand Rapids: Zondervan Publishing House, 1978), p. 119.

such groans come from him as never came from human breast before. I look upon the earth and see it red with his blood, while his face is smeared with gory sweat, and I pray to myself, "My God, my Savior, what aileth thee?" I hear him reply, "I am suffering for thy sin."[48]

As the bearer of man's sins, the Lord was entirely immersed in sorrow and woe. His was sorrow of the highest degree, "even to the point of death." No mortal man could have endured and lived through this kind of sorrow. At Calvary Christ's physical suffering was prominent; but at Gethsemane the physical was subordinate to the intense mental and spiritual suffering. Jesus prayed, "My Father, if it is possible, may this cup be taken from me." It was not the prospect of pain and death that tormented our Lord in the Garden, but the isolation from God and the sense of forsakenness. It was the whole shadow of the cross, with its spiritual darkness and desolation, the bearing of the burden of human sin and dread of separation from His Father that He struggled against. That was the critical hour; nevertheless, the Lord Jesus said, "Not as I will, but as you will." Although He had a full and clear sense of the bitter sufferings that lay before Him, He was willing to submit to them out of obedience to the Father's will, His purpose of redemption. Here we see the ultimate rejection of the root of sin and the error of selfism. Self is the root of sin. If we trace human sin to its ultimate source, we will arrive at self. The essence of all sin is the assertion of one's will against God's.

Judas and his band had come to apprehend Jesus in the Garden of Gethsemane (Matthew 26:47-56; Mark 14:43-50; Luke 22:47-53; John 18:1-11). Jesus showed His divine knowledge and almighty power when He spoke the words, "I am he." The bank of soldiers drew back and fell to the ground (John 18:6). Then Jesus meekly yielded Himself to suffer and die. One word and all of them could have been consumed by His power

---

48 Charles H. Spurgeon, *The Treasury of Spurgeon on the Life and Works of our Lord,* vol. 6 (Grand Rapids: Baker Book House, 1979), p. 131.

and killed. But Jesus would not speak a word to protect Himself, for He came to lay down His life for His sheep. Christ's spirit of self-sacrifice is also seen in His concern for His disciples: "If you are looking for me, then let these men go" (John 18:8). One would not expect a man who was experiencing the grief that Jesus was feeling to remember others; yet, even in His darkest hour His concern was not for Himself. Here is a picture of Christ's mission of deliverance. When He said, "Let these men go," He was foreshadowing His own substitutive work for which He came into the world. Peter, who was always impetuous, had drawn his sword and had struck a servant of the high priest, cutting off his ear. Jesus came forward in all His gentleness and "answered, 'No more of this!' And He touched the man's ear and healed Him" (Luke 22:51). Then Jesus uttered the words: "Do you think I cannot call on my Father, and he will at once put at my disposal more than twelve legions of angels? But how then would the Scriptures be fulfilled that say it must happen in this way?" (Matthew 26:53-54). Jesus had at His disposal the means of self-defense, but he refrained from using it. We saw Him betrayed into the hands of sinners; He had to die, and so Christ went with them willingly. Jesus did not die because He lacked the strength and power to defend Himself. He died because He willingly surrendered Himself to make propitiation. Christ Jesus was so perfectly submissive and eager to secure men's salvation that He refused to pray even for His own relief: "Shall I not drink the cup the Father has given me?" (John 18:11). His Father's will was that He should suffer. He would not do anything that would oppose it. C. H. Spurgeon writes:

> The crucifixion of Jesus Christ was the crowning sin of the human race. In his death we shall find all the sins of mankind uniting in foul conspiracy. Envy and pride and hate are there, with covetousness, falsehood, and blasphemy, eager to rush on to cruelty, revenge, and murder.[49]

---

49 *Ibid.*, p. 383.

The incarnation of the Lord was a wonderful act of humiliation, but the voluntary abasement that would take Him to the cross was even more wonderful and mysterious than that. To humble Himself and become human and to dwell in a body were astonishing enough, but then to die for such loathsome human creatures is incomprehensible. We see Christ's selflessness and submissiveness as He moved toward His cross. He was the Master over all circumstances and all men. Although there were times when circumstances seemed to have mastered Him, He was sovereign over them all. Christ moved calmly and with definite intent toward the cross. Christ's enemies were also moving toward the cross. In their final gathering with Pilate, they had successfully obtained a sentence of death by crucifixion for Jesus. G. Campbell Morgan writes, "Grace and sin were moving toward the same sad end; grace in the person of God's King planning for the cross; sin in the person of the rulers plotting for the cross."[50] With shameless enthusiasm, the wicked bound His hands. The Omnipotent was bound; how low He stooped! They spat in Christ's face and struck Him with their fists. God's own Son was despised, reviled, thorn-crowned, scourged, and led out to be crucified. Morgan continues:

> Let us remember that our Lord's weakness was undertaken for our sakes . . . . Therefore it is the more painful for us to see that this voluntary humiliation of himself must be made the object of so much derision and scorn, though worthy of the utmost praise. He stoops to save us, and we laugh at him as he stoops; he leaves the throne that he may lift us up to it, but while he is graciously descending, the hoarse laughter of an ungodly world is his only reward.[51]

---

50 G. Campbell Morgan, *The Gospel According to Matthew*, vol. 6 (New York: Fleming H. Revell, n.d.), p. 298.

51 *Ibid.*, p. 407.

In all of this Jesus did not say a word. He prayed, but He did not pray that His Father would remember their vicious crime against Him; instead He prayed for them. He pleaded for His murderers, "Father, forgive them, for they do not know what they are doing" (Luke 23:34). What marvelous self-forgetfulness! What almighty love! Jesus prayed for His killers when they would not even pray for themselves.

As He hung on the cross, Christ's words to the dying thief provided another of the endless examples of Christ's selflessness. Those words demonstrated not only His power to save, but also His willingness to save all those who would come to Him in faith. Remember, our Lord was at His lowest. Christ hung there, stripped of his clothing, nailed to a cross, dying in agony; yet, while His life was ebbing away, He saved a convicted felon. With all of love's compassion and composure, Christ Jesus spoke His words of comfort to this newly awakened sinner: "Today you will be with me in paradise" (Luke 23:43).

The Bible describes a darkness that fell over the face of the earth. Out of that darkness Jesus cried out in a loud voice, "My God, my God, why have you forsaken me?" (Matthew 27:46; Mark 15:34). Those words were spoken at the greatest point of Christ's anguish, the lowest pit of misery and grief. His work was almost done. Spurgeon writes, "You shall measure the height of his love, if it be ever measured, by the depth of his grief, it that can ever be known."[52] That Christ was forsaken by His Father was the most grievous of all His sufferings. He had never asked Pilate's guards, "Why do you flog me?" or his soldiers, "Why do you hit me, spit on me, and nail me to a cross?" But when His Father turned His back on His only begotten Son, He cried out with a loud voice . . . "Why . . . .?" What a high price He paid to redeem us from the curse of the law! A grieving heart is the worst kind of misery, but a man can endure the worst distress and depression of soul if he has his God to go to and comfort him. He also can bear a wounded or sickly body. But man's consciousness that he has been deserted by God is beyond comprehension. It

---

52 *Ibid.*, p. 535.

is unendurable. Christ indeed was alone. All had forsaken Him, even His own God. Why did God forsake His Son? There is nothing in Christ that God should forsake Him, for Christ was perfectly sinless. The answer to the question is man's sin. Christ, the lover of men's souls, became the Great Sacrifice.

There were many spectators at the crucifixion. Some that were present were sympathetic, most were indifferent and curious, but many scorned, ridiculed, and insulted Him. "Those who passed by hurled insults at him, shaking their heads" (Mark 15:29). Mockery was a bitter ingredient in the Lord's cup of sorrow. He had been mocked by the servants of the high priest and by Herod and his soldiers. Then, as He hung dying, one would imagine He would be pitied and left alone; but the cruelty intensified. This brutality had been prophesied (Psalm 22:6-8). Jesus Himself had often predicted His own sufferings. They were part of the working out of the plan of redemption. He would suffer scorn and contempt, as well as bodily pain. To many of the spectators gathered there, He was a poor, miserable, and helpless man, whose claims were so outrageous that they laughed at and ridiculed Him. They said, "He saved others, but he can't save himself" (Mark 15:31). Although they were ignorant, they proclaimed a great truth. If Jesus was to save others, then He could not save Himself. He could have saved Himself, but He forgot Himself for their sakes. He gave Himself up voluntarily.

Why did the Lord Jesus Christ not focus on His own glory? The answer to that question is found in Christ's loving determination to suffer for the sins of His people. In Christ's love for them, believers find our deepest job. Paul calls the relationship between Christ and His church a "profound mystery" (Ephesians 5:32). There is much we do not understand about this marvelous union of believers with Jesus, but it is a mystery of boundless love. He loves His people infinitely. They are the objects of His love, for He said, "Love each other as I have loved you" (John 15:12). Jesus' disciples could have inferred by His many acts of love that He loved them, but Jesus did not leave it to an inference. Jesus deliberately and openly declared His love.

As if to confirm this beyond all doubt, the Lord compared His love for His disciples with a most extraordinary kind of love; the love His Father has for Him. Jesus said, "As the Father has loved me, so I have loved you" (John 15:9). No Christian would ever dare to doubt the love of the Father for His Son; therefore, they may be confident that He loves them.

True love, which is God's love, is others-oriented. God's love "is not self-seeking" (1 Corinthians 13:5). The Lord did not set His love on His disciples because there was anything worthy in them. Paul writes: "For he chose us in him before the creation of the world" (Ephesians 1:4). The reason for His choice was love. He loved them because He loved them. God Himself is the fountain of love. The men that arrested and bound Jesus did not know that He was the Almighty God. They did not know that "By Him all things were created in heaven and earth, visible and invisible, whether thrones or powers or rulers or authorities . . . ." (Colossians 1:16). They did not realize that while He hung on the cross in apparent weakness, He was nevertheless upholding all things by His power (Hebrews 1:3). How truly amazing that Christ Jesus, Who is able to uphold all things or destroy all things, was held captive. Jesus, whom the angels adore, took upon Himself human nature and sank so low as to submit Himself to the most cruel and barbarous of men. His power never proved itself more powerful than when He restrained Himself, for love's sake, and endured the brutish treatment of mankind. All human knowledge is lost in mystery and adoration of this love that Christ Jesus has for His chosen. He veiled His deity and did not focus on His glory. It was love at its utmost.

The Lord was willing from the very beginning to be a Savior. He was willing to come in the likeness of sinful men and be born in Bethlehem. He was willing to be beaten, spat upon, ridiculed, crucified, and killed as the worst of criminals. "With a loud cry, Jesus breathed his last" (Mark 15:37). He freely gave up His life; He could have kept it. It was not taken from Him by any power superior to His own. Jesus willingly bore man's sin in perfect submission to the Father's will. He had such a desire to save men, such a thirst to do the Father's will that He refused to prevent His sufferings by prayer. Who else, He asked, could drink this cup? He was not constrained; instead, there was selfless love.

When Christ began to preach, He gathered disciples who would also become preachers. He called them to follow Him, saying, "Come, follow me and I will make you fishers of men" (Matthew 4:19). Jesus did not say, "Follow me for what you can get out of it," or "Follow me and make something of yourself." Instead he said, "Follow me and I will make something out of you." Christ, who was always others-oriented, would make His disciples a blessing to others. So, "at once they left their nets" (Matthew 4:20). They forsook their livelihoods and homes, not for a more profitable (monetarily) position, but for a less profitable one. The disciples were poor fishermen, whose only possessions were their boats and nets, from which they earned a meager living. Having forsaken these tools of their livelihood, they were even poorer. Then, three years later, the risen Lord called the disciples together, gave them His final instructions, and sent them out on their own (Matthew 28:16-20). They would be missionaries and would preach the gospel to all the nations. Theirs would be a difficult and dangerous task. The apostles had to be content to bear the cross and follow their Lord, Who bore the cross for them and died for their salvation. They were to win men's souls and teach them the ways and the words of the Lord – words such as "Blessed are the poor in spirit . . . the meek . . . the merciful . . . let your light shine for all to see . . . love your enemies . . . whoever humbles himself like this little child is greatest . . . and love is not self-seeking." In other words, the apostles were to teach their disciples to be others-oriented, as Christ was others-oriented. When He was about to leave them, they were deeply saddened. Christ's farewell words, "And surely I am with you always, to the very end of the age" (Matthew 28:20), were full of sympathy, love, and comfort to them. He promised the disciples His spiritual presence, which would sustain them in the difficulties and sufferings that were to come. Just as we saw our Lord Jesus Christ in His agony, we also saw Him in His risen glory, oblivious to self, thinking of the welfare of others.

Chapter Three
The Miracles of Jesus Christ

Illustrations of Jesus' others-oriented way of life are also seen in His miracles. Men were slow to believe Christ's words; therefore, His words were confirmed by His works. Jesus performed miracles that men might see with their eyes that the power of God was upon Him, and might know that He spoke with divine authority. There was a direct correlation between what Jesus did and what He taught: what Jesus did confirmed what He taught. The things the Lord taught explained what He did. There was never a time when Jesus ever said, "Do as I say but not as I do."

There was another aspect to Christ's miracles. Jesus' miracles reflected His others-oriented character, which was naturally expressed by His love and sympathy for suffering mankind. For example, a distressed father (a nobleman) whose son was sick with a deadly fever, journeyed to Cana to solicit the help of this Miracle Worker (John 4:46-54). He had consulted every physician within his reach, and all of them candidly pronounced the boy hopeless. He recalled the stories he had heard of the miraculous cures performed by Jesus of Nazareth. The Lord's reputation as One Who was both able and willing to cure illnesses had spread. And so this grieving father, whose faith was small and whose understanding was limited, thought that Jesus must be present to heal the child and so pleaded, "Sir, come down before my child dies." The Master looked upon him with kindness and compassion; and in spite of the nobleman's weak faith and slowness of understanding, He freely granted his request. Jesus simply spoke the words, "Your son will live" (John 4:50). With every act of benevolence we are reminded of Doctor Luke's description of this Miracle Worker as One Who went about doing good and healing all who were under the power of the devil (Acts 10:38).

The incompatibility of Jesus' others-oriented way of life with that of the self-theorists is seen in a series of miracles in what is commonly referred to as the year of Jesus' popularity. First, there was the miracle of cleansing of the leper (Matthew 8:1-4; Mark 1:40-45; Luke 5:12-14). Matthew placed this miracle immediately after the Sermon on the Mount. There was a leper who had heard of Jesus and perhaps, on the edge of the crowd, had heard him speak. Leprosy was a loathsome, miserable, and disfiguring disease. The man was probably in the advanced stages of this terrible disease, for he was "covered with leprosy" (Luke 5:12). His skin and bones were rotting, and most likely his fingers, teeth, and hair were gone. A leper lived alone outside the city gates and was cut off from society and family. He had no one who could give him any consolation. This particular leper came and knelt before Jesus and said, "Lord, if you are willing, you can make me clean" (Matthew 8:2). Spurgeon writes:

> Our Lord saw to it that he came not in vain. Poor soul! . . . our Lord rewarded him with his sympathy. He looked at him with a different look from what the leper had ever received before. When others glanced at the leper they went by as quickly as they could . . . ghastly spectacle. Nobody pitied lepers in those days, for they judged them to be smitten of God. But when Jesus saw the afflicted man . . . "he was moved with compassion."[53]

When Jesus saw the leper at His feet, He was overcome with emotion. Jesus' words, "I am willing" (Matthew 8:3), were an expression of His sympathy, kindness, mercy, and grace. Immediately Christ's hand went out, and He touched the man and healed him. The leper had not expected such an act of condescension, for no one else would have defiled himself by touching a leper. While others drew back in horror and evaded the leper, Jesus touched him to do him good.

---

53 Charles Haddon Spurgeon, *A Treasury of Spurgeon on the Life and Works of Our Lord,* vol. 4 (Grand Rapids: Baker Book House, 1979), p. 157.

Also worthy of our consideration is the account of the healing of the Roman centurion's servant. The one thing which gave the centurion a place in the Holy Scriptures was his humility and selflessness. This man had deep insight into his own heart and learned to see sin in its true colors. He said, "Lord, I do not deserve to have you come under my roof. But just say the words, and my servant will be healed" (Matthew 8:5-13; Luke 7:1-10). There are no words that can exaggerate man's sinful condition. There are no feelings that a man can experience that can portray the true condition of his heart. No man is worthy that Christ should come to him, neither is any man admirable enough to draw near to Christ. Of course, this idea is contrary to that of the self-theorist who espouses man's inner goodness, which is based on the humanistic-evolutionary model. The Christian self-theorist disagrees with the humanistic view which espouses that there is no God. However, he would agree with the humanist and preserve the idea, which is logical to the evolutionary model but contrary to the Bible, that man possesses inner goodness and worth. For example, Christian author Josh McDowell says man has "tremendous worth" and is "delightful to God, lovable, worthy, and competent."[54] Similarly, Christian author Anthony Hoekema, who writes about the importance of self-esteem, says, "Surely God would not give His Son for creatures He considered to be of little worth![55] But the Bible teaches that is exactly what God did. Hoekema continues by blaming evangelical pastors for all the problems that low self-esteem is said to cause because they are continually reminding people of their depravity and sin.

The centurion felt that he was unworthy, but Christ esteemed his contrite and humble spirit. Again, Spurgeon writes, "Humility is healthy; lowliness is no disease. When one thinks worse and worse of oneself, one is getting nearer and nearer to the truth. Men are by nature depraved, degraded,

---

54 Josh McDowell, *Building Your Self-Image* (Wheaton: Tyndale House, 1978), pp. 21, 24.
55 Anthony Hoekema, *The Christian Looks at Himself* (Grand Rapids: William B. Eerdmans, n.d.), pp. 16, 22.

guilty, and worthy of the wrath of God."[56]   The Bible says that the centurion "astonished" the Lord. Contrary to selfism, which finds virtue in the man who loves himself, our Lord praised the man for his great faith: "I tell you the truth, I have not found anyone in Israel with such great faith" (Matthew 8:10). The more a man perceives the glories of Jesus Christ the Lord, the humbler he will be. One's knowledge of his nothingness leads to greater and greater faith. What a marvelous opportunity the Lord would have had in His encounter with the centurion to expound the virtues and positive aspects of self-esteem. What an act of kindness Christ would have modeled by gently rebuking this man for his "unhealthy" attitude, which according to the advocates of self-love is "at the root of almost every one of our personal problems."[57] If the centurion's low self-estimate was so damaging to himself and his relationship with God and others, surely Jesus, who was always concerned about relationships, would have corrected his fallacious view.   But that was not the case, for we have learned that self-love was the tyrant that brought sin and sickness into the world. Of course, the supreme example of humility is Jesus Christ, Who laid aside the splendor of His heavenly majesty and with cheerful willingness came to earth to do good to a centurion's servant. Jesus granted more to the centurion than he had asked. The request was, "Just say the word and my servant will be healed" (Matthew 8:8). Jesus' tender reply was, "I will go and heal him" (v 7). The true blessings are for those who, like Jesus, are others-oriented.

On another occasion we see Christ's others-oriented way of living when He healed Peter's mother-in-law (Matthew 8:14-17; Mark 1:29-24; Luke 4:38-41). The Lord Jesus Christ was at the end of a long and heavy day. He had preached in the synagogue and had performed miracles among a great crowd of people. At last it was time for Him to rest and refresh Himself with a night's sleep. But as they entered Peter's house,

---

56 Charles H. Spurgeon, *A Treasury of Spurgeon on the Life and Works of Our Lord,* vol. 4 (Grand Rapids: Baker Book House, 1979), p. 487.

57 Robert Schuller, *Self-Love* (New York: Jove Books, 1978), p. 9.

they found another work of mercy to perform. Peter's mother-in-law was sick with a terrible fever. Jesus went to her room, and, having pity on her, He rebuked the fever. Jesus lifted her gently up by the hand, and she found herself perfectly restored to health. The news then spread quickly of her healing, and many sick and demon-possessed were brought to Him. As tired as Jesus was, He selflessly healed them all. In Matthew we read about Christ's acts of sympathy taken from the ancient prophecy of the "Servant of the Lord" (Isaiah 53): "Surely he took up our infirmities and carried our sorrows" (Isaiah 53:4). Christ did not literally take upon Himself the sickness, fevers and pains He healed. Rather, Jesus empathized with individuals in their infirmities. Christ bore their diseases and pains as a burden on His compassionate heart. In other words, the Lord suffered with those who suffered. His healing power was directly related to His power to sympathize.

The miracle of Christ's calming the storm on the Sea of Galilee occurred the same evening that He had healed Peter's mother-in-law (Matthew 8:23-27; Mark 4:36-41). Christ had been teaching from a boat and had given orders to His disciples to sail to the other side of the sea into the country of Gadara. Christ, who was always thinking of others, in His foreknowledge was preparing to meet a pitiful man who was possessed with a legion of devils. As they sailed on the smooth waters, Jesus, who was exhausted after a long day of ministry, had fallen asleep. But their trip across the lake was not ordained to be a pleasant one. Without warning, a great storm swept down from the hills with such violence that even the experienced fishermen feared for their lives. Christ could have prevented the storm, and they could have sailed peacefully across the lake. But for their sakes Jesus sent the storm, and then He delivered them from it in order to increase their faith (see John 11:4; Hebrews 12:11; Romans 8:28-29). Matthew Henry writes, "He slept at this time, to try the faith of his disciples, whether they could trust him when he seemed to slight them. He slept not so much with a desire to be refreshed, as with a design to be awakened."[58]

Christ then calmed the sea. So the disciples and their Master approached the shore peacefully, but another storm confronted them: "Two demon-possessed men coming from the tombs met him" (Matthew 8:28-34; Mark 5:1-20; Luke 8:26-37). Mark and Luke mention only the one man who was described as being possessed by a legion of evil spirits. This man's case was very extraordinary. He lived naked among the tombs. The authorities had failed to constrain him for his own protection, as well as for the protection of others who lived nearby. This poor man was continually tormented. Mark explains, "Night and day among the tombs and in the hills he would cry out and cut himself with stones" (Mark 5:5). By grace the Lord Jesus worked a mighty miracle in the man. The Lord commanded the evil spirits to "go." What a wonderful description we have of the delivered demoniac, who was "sitting at Jesus' feet, dressed and in his right mind" (Luke 8:35). Jesus was always others-oriented, and He taught the man who had been demon-possessed to be others-oriented. As Jesus was entering the boat to return to the other side, He said to him, "Go home to your family and tell them how much the Lord has done for you and how he has had mercy on you" (Mark 5:19). In other words, he was to glorify God and care for the souls of his family and countrymen.

In Capernaum the Lord was known as the great Preacher, the loving and compassionate Healer. Four friends carried their hopelessly paralyzed neighbor through the streets, hoping that he would be healed by Jesus (Matthew 9:1-8; Mark 2:3-12; Luke 5:18-26). The great crowd surrounding the house made their entry through the front door impossible. After sizing up the situation, the bearers carried the paralyzed man up the stairs to the roof and lowered him down right in front of Jesus, who was preaching to the people. Jesus paused. The crowd, astonished at the inappropriateness of such an action, looked inquisitively at Christ. Jesus, however, was not offended. He was pleased

---

58 Matthew Henry, *Commentary*, vol.5 (Old Tappan: Fleming H. Revell, n.d.) p. 110.

and quickly responded to the faith of the four bearers and their helpless friend by saying, "Your sins are forgiven." With these words Christ publicly pronounced His divine commission. He declared that He had the power to forgive sins. Forgiving sins was what He came to do, and He delighted to do it. Christ's business, bliss, and glory was to pardon sin. The paralytic's bodily weakness was secondary compared to the spiritual paralysis of sin.

While his friends thought only of his physical disease, the great Physician's penetrating eyes saw through the superficial symptoms and into the disease itself. Jesus never forgave where there was no repentance. There was no universal granting of forgiveness. There had to be a consciousness and confession of sin. When man sinned, God could have instantly destroyed our rebellious race, but He did not. Instead, the Son of God became son of Mary, subjected to pain, weakness, poverty, and shame in order to redeem sinful men. The Lord gave the poor paralytic man much more than he had asked. The man asked Jesus to heal him, and Jesus did heal his body; but the man received infinitely more when Jesus cleansed him from his sins. When the Lord raised this paralyzed man from his mat, He did not do it just to let the man himself know that his sins were forgiven; the man knew that already. There were others that Jesus cared for, and He longed that they too should have faith in Him for spiritual healing. Christ's focus was then on the Scribes and Pharisees; and with words of mercy and love toward them, He said, "But so that you may know that the Son of Man has authority on earth to forgive sins [he said to the paralyzed man], get up, take your mat and go home" (Matthew 9:6; Luke 5:24).

The miracle of the Lord's healing the bleeding woman occurred while He was on the road to Jairus' house to raise his daughter. So we have a miracle within a miracle. This demonstrates Christ's overflowing grace toward others, in that as He went to do good to one He paused to do good to another. Jairus, a distressed father, had bowed before the Lord and presented a heart-felt plea for his dying twelve-year-old daughter. Immediately Jesus left to go to Jairus' house but was interrupted by a woman who had been afflicted by a disease for twelve long years (Matthew 9:20-22). All her money had been spent in a fruitless search for a cure. She was no better but, in fact, was getting worse. Her condition was painful, distressing, and seemingly hopeless. But what she had heard and had seen concerning Jesus made her sure of His superabundant power and sympathy to heal the sick. A touch would do. Jesus was so full of power that just a touch of the "edge of his cloak" would be sufficient. Virtue and grace so saturated the Lord that they seemingly ran down His garments. The woman thought to herself, "If only I could touch a thread from His robe I would be healed." The woman was among the mass of people who were following Jesus to Jairus' house. With the energy of despair, she maneuvered her way through the crowd, timidly touched the hem of Jesus' robe, and was immediately healed of her infirmity. But Jesus felt her presence, and He knew about her trouble and her faith. By an act of Jesus' will, power went forth from Him and healed her sickness.

Many people had touched the Lord as He went on His way, but one touched Him with the hand of faith. That touch Jesus knew at once. "Who touched my clothes?" the Lord asked. He looked around until His loving eyes met the woman's eyes. The woman was overwhelmed with shame and embarrassment. Jesus, who understood perfectly and truly sympathized, addressed her with the utmost kindness, "Take heart, daughter," he said, "your faith has healed you." The Lord's words convey to each person that she is not lost in the crowd. It's not just that God loves mankind, but God loves each man personally. The disciples saw a throng of people, while Jesus saw a poor grieving woman. Encouraged by Jesus' tenderness, the woman made her confession before all that were present: "Then the woman, knowing what had happened to her, came and fell at his feet and, trembling with fear, told him the whole truth" (Mark 5:33).

As for Jairus, his faith was being severely tested. He had gone to the Savior and told Him that his daughter was at the point of death. Christ immediately consented to go to her bedside. To Jairus, time was critical. But Jesus, who never failed to respond to need, stopped along the way and healed the bleeding woman. What parent does not understand the feelings that Jairus must have experienced? His little daughter was dying, and he had to stand by as Jesus conversed with the woman about her sickness. Moments later, some men came from Jairus' house and informed him that his daughter was dead. Jesus met their sad message with an encouraging one: "Don't be afraid, just believe, and she will be healed" (Luke 8:50). With this word of hope Christ entered the room where the little girl laid and, with His usual tenderness, Jesus took her by the hand and said, "My child, get up!" Then, with His typical thoughtfulness, Jesus told her parents to give her something to eat. Jesus was always concerned with the temporal needs of individuals.

But the day's work was not yet over for our Lord. Before Jesus retired for the evening, He would heal two blind men and cast a demon out of another (Matthew 9:27-34). As Jesus was returning from the house of Jairus, two blind men pleading to be healed followed after Him. They expressed their faith when they called Jesus the Son of David, a Messianic title. Since prophecy declared that the Messiah was to open blind eyes, they reasoned that Jesus could open their blind eyes. The men appealed to Jesus to perform the signs of His office, and in doing so they honored Him with a real and practical faith. Jesus ignored their first plea in order to test their faith. The Lord was always concerned with men's faith. He always dealt with men in such a way that they themselves would know their faith and that their faith would be strengthened. Jesus cared about men's relationships with God, in which faith is essential. Faith is that which forms a connection between man's soul and the Lord Jesus Christ. Christ did not heal them publicly in the streets, but "When he had gone indoors, the blind men came to him" (v. 28). What a wonderful picture of the Lord's desire to relieve the sufferings of men! Seeming almost rude, the men uninvited pressed their way through the door and into the house. But Christ's door was always open to believing and importunate people. Although Jesus was tired from the long day, His tenderness was obvious, and the blind men were welcomed, rather than considered thoughtless and rude.

The second miracle that Jesus performed, after He departed from Jairus' house, was the healing of the dumb demoniac. This poor man did not come on his own but was brought to Jesus by his friends. He was helpless under the power of the evil one. He could not speak. They brought him in just as the blind man went out. We see again how selfless the Lord was. Even though Jesus was weary from his long day, He never wearied of doing good to others. When the man was brought before Christ, neither a word was spoken nor was a request made on his behalf. The Lord perceived his condition to be the work of the devil. Divine mercy did not delay even a minute to rescue the man from his suffering. Christ Jesus cast the demon out, and the man spoke.

The day after he had cured the centurion's servant, Christ raised to life a widow's son at Nain (Luke 7:11-17). The Savior was journeying and working miracles while He was on the road. No time and no place could find Jesus unwilling or unable to help those in need. The seemingly incidental meeting of Jesus and His disciples with the funeral procession was deeply rooted in the councils of divine providence. This meeting at the gate, as the crowds brought the young man out to bury him, was no accident; it was prearranged so that Christ the Lord could show the readiness and naturalness of the operations of His life-giving power. Luke writes, "When the Lord saw her, His heart went out to her and He said, 'Don't cry'" (Luke 7:13). Then Jesus touched the coffin and commanded the young man to "get up." This was so spontaneous that Jesus seemed as if He could not help raising him from the dead. What great compassion was compressed into those two simple but authoritative words, "Don't cry." Christ showed both His pity and His power in raising the widow's son to life. When Jesus saw the broken and weeping mother following her son to the grave, He had compassion upon her. No request was made to Jesus for help; purely out of the goodness of His heart He was grieved for her and raised her son.

One Sabbath, Jesus entered the synagogue; a man with a shriveled hand was in the congregation that day. The Pharisees pointed him out to Christ, not because they were sympathetic toward the man, but because they hated Christ and had conspired to find some fault by which they could accuse Him of breaking the Sabbath. The fact that they pointed the man out to Christ was a tribute to the Lord's selfless and compassionate reputation. They knew Jesus would not pass by this poor man without helping him. Jesus knew their thoughts. Mark describes the Savior as looking "round about on them with anger, being grieved for the hardness of their hearts" (Mark 3:5) as he healed the man. Jesus' feelings were mixed toward the Pharisees, who persisted venomously in their opposition toward Him. There was anger, grief, indignation, and sorrow because of the hardness of their hearts. They were willfully blind to all Christ had taught and performed. Christ was angry at their sin; nevertheless, He was still compassionate toward them as sinners. Christ knew that the hardness of their hearts would one day bring them face to face with divine justice. Foreseeing their coming misery and grief, He grieved for them. They were destroying themselves by their hatred for Jesus, and this would ultimately lead to their ruin. They would not let Christ bless them; therefore, He was angry and grieved.

Christ, though He resided in Galilee, went up to Jerusalem to a Jewish feast. Near the Sheep Gate there was a pool where "A great number of disabled people used to lie—the blind, the lame, the paralyzed." Here Jesus healed a man who had been crippled for thirty-eight years (John 5:1-20). Once again, we observe that Jesus was others-oriented; His focus was always on others. It was the Sabbath. Where and how had Jesus spent His day? He could have spent a pleasurable afternoon with Mary, Martha, and Lazarus in Bethany. Jesus could have been asked to dine at the home of some disciple who lived in Jerusalem. Surely there would have been ample opportunities for the Savior had He desired to spend the day among friends. Where was Christ found on this holiday? Jesus was found where He was most wanted and where He might do the most good. The Lord spent the feast day with the blind, the lame, and the paralyzed. Jesus feasted on doing good to others. Because He was the incarnation of mercy, Jesus was naturally attracted to this place of misery and pain. The scene excited Jesus' compassion and reminded Him of a more terrible malady, that of sin, which He came to take away. The crippled man was in the grip of utter despair, but Jesus' question, "Do you want to get well?" (John 5:6), fanned the smoldering embers of faith. Jesus was always concerned with a person's faith. His question was designed to redirect the man's mind from the pool of water to the Living Water. Then came the command, "Get up! Pick up your mat and walk" (v. 8). Christ's divine words were accompanied by divine power: "At once the man was cured; he picked up his mat and walked."

The year of popularity had ended; the year of opposition had begun. It was a dangerous time in the life of the Lord. Herod was suspicious of Him, the Pharisees' hostility was no longer concealed, and the people, who had been enthusiastic over His teachings and wonderful works, were now deeply offended at some of His words.

Consider the miracle of the feeding of the five thousand (Matthew 14:13-21; Mark 6:32-44; Luke 9:10-17; John 6:1-13). When Jesus heard of the death of John the Baptist, He "withdrew by boat privately to a solitary place" (Matthew 14:13) on the eastern side of the lake for a time of seclusion. The privacy Jesus craved was short-lived; however, He did not complain. The people followed, and "When Jesus landed, and saw a large crowd, he had compassion on them and healed their sick" (v. 14). The Savior always considered others before Himself. The crowd showed very little consideration for Jesus, but His gracious and humble spirit was ever ready to show the fullest consideration for them. Jesus' sympathies prevailed over His search for solitude. The apostle Paul writes, "We who are strong ought to bear with the failings of the weak and not to please ourselves. Each of us should please his neighbor for his good, to build him up. For even Christ did not please himself" (Romans 15:1-2). Later that evening, the sight of the weary multitude touched Jesus' heart; they were all far from home and had no food to eat. Christ's motive was compassion. This was the motive that brought Him from heaven to do His atoning work. He came into the world because He took pity on the world's misery. Jesus asked Philip where He might go to buy bread to feed the hungry crowd, but Jesus "asked this only to test him, for he already had in mind what he was going to do" (John 6:6). Jesus never queried His disciples about their self-esteem. He never asked the kind of questions that are so frequently asked today: "How do you feel about yourself?" "How is your self-image?" "Do you love yourself?" He always inquired in some fashion about their faith. Jesus taught them to be others-oriented—in other words, to have faith in Him. Jesus did not want food from Philip, but faith. The disciples, with their heartlessness and lack of faith, would have driven the needy crowds away. But Jesus gave the command for the people to sit down, and with "five small barley loaves and two small fish" (v. 9) he fed five thousand hungry people.

After the miracles of the loaves, Jesus immediately "made the disciples get into a boat and go ahead of Him to the other side, while He dismissed the crowd" (Matthew 14:22). The reason for this hasty breaking up of the multitude was because the people, affected by the miracles of the loaves, were about to take Jesus by force and make Him a King. But Jesus was not blinded by the popular excitement. He was King, but His kingdom was to come in God's appointed way, the cross. Jesus instead retired to the mountain for solitude and prayer. He prayed late into the night.

Meanwhile, out on the lake, the disciples were "straining at the oars." A sudden and furious storm had made their crossing difficult. Several hours had gone by, and they were only halfway across the lake. From the mountain top where Jesus had gone to pray He saw the danger His disciples were experiencing. Herbert Lockyer says that Jesus:

> . . . saw them in the darkest hour of their extremity. In His solitude, the Eternal Being was watching the little specks of boats and was cognizant of the sore trouble of their toil. Buffeted by those contrary winds, the disciples were to learn of the Master's divine sympathy and of His willingness to enter the struggle.[59]

They had spent hours in the storm, and they thought Jesus was neglecting them. Then, "about the fourth watch of the night he went out to them, walking on the lake" (Mark 6:48). Lockyer comments, "Though He would not fling Himself from the Temple pinnacle for self-glory, He flung Himself on the waves to reassure His own that He was near."[60] The Lord came to His people in their time of greatest need and spoke words of comfort: "Take courage, it is I. Don't be afraid" (Matthew 14:27). The ever impulsive Peter, over-estimating his faith and perhaps thinking too much of self (as all men are prone to do) stepped out onto the waves. Peter stepped out at the Lord's bidding. Jesus was probably teaching Peter his own weakness and the danger of presumption. With his eyes on Jesus, Peter took a few steps and then began to sink. "Lord, save me!" he cried (v. 30). Peter's prayer was a prayer of penitence and self-abasement. The trial had taught Peter a lesson concerning faith. "Because the Lord disciplines those he loves" (Hebrews 12:6), Christ gently rebuked Peter, "You of little faith, why did you doubt" (Matthew 14:31). Jesus entered the boat and, instantly, all was calm.

The Lord then left Galilee where He had been teaching for (perhaps) two years. At first there had been a time of dazzling popularity, but His popularity had excited the intense hostility of the Pharisees. He was threatening their influence, and so they

---

59 Herbert Lockyer, *All the Miracles of the Bible* (Grand Rapids: Zondervan Publishing House, 1961), p. 201.

60 *Ibid.*, p. 202.

conspired against Him. On one occasion the Lord traveled to the borders of Tyre and Sidon, in prudence rather than fear, for a time of rest. "He entered a house and did not want anyone to know it; yet he could not keep his presence a secret" (Mark 7:24). A Canaanite woman sought Him out with an eager intrusiveness that was only justified by the greatness and pressing nature of her need. She had a "little daughter" who was possessed by an evil spirit. Jesus, who had an endless reserve of mercy, healed her daughter, but not before He tried her faith by His silence and discouraging replies. In the testing of the woman's faith, we are again reminded of Jesus' others-oriented nature. Being omniscient, the Savior knew her well. He knew that she could stand the trial and would greatly benefit by it. Jesus also knew that He would be glorified by her faith throughout the ages. Jesus concealed His tender compassion for the poor woman under the disguise of indifference. Jesus in His wisdom tried her, while at the same time His grace sustained her. The trial prompted her deep feelings of humility and trust. She was trained by Jesus' sarcasm and indifference. Christ's methods of increasing faith were prompted by love, with the intent of eliciting love. The Lord admired the faith of this Canaanite woman just as He had marveled at the faith of the Gentile centurion.

The miracle of the feeding of the four thousand demonstrates the fact that God knows what His people need before they ask Him (Matthew 15:29-38; Mark 8:1-10). Christ had gone up into a mountain, but again He could not hide: "Great crowds came to him, bringing the lame, the blind, the crippled, the mute and many others, and laid them at his feet; and he healed them." On the third day the people were very hungry. Many of the people had come from far away, and their food was gone. Jesus called His disciples together and said, "I have compassion for these people." Jesus cared for them. He cared not only for their present condition of hunger but also for the suffering it would bring if He did not feed them. Christ said, "I do not want to send them away hungry, or they may collapse on the way." On this our tender-hearted Lord could not bear to think. We cannot overlook the fact that our Savior demonstrated His miraculous power not to answer a challenge, nor to prove His divine authority, as so often before, but simply to show loving compassion for someone. Jesus commanded the people to seat themselves in an orderly fashion; and then with seven loaves of bread and a few small fish Jesus fed the crowd until they were all filled. The thoughtful kindness of Jesus in refusing to send the people away tired and hungry, teaches us that He is a kind, considerate, and ever-watchful Provider. We must not forget His example when He gave thanks. He modeled that one should always focus on God for the blessings He gives.

On another occasion, Jesus was about to be stoned by the Jews. He withdrew and passed through the crowd, not in a hurried manner, but in a calm and dignified way. The moment after, when Jesus was sufficiently out of range to be unobserved, He fixed His eyes upon a blind beggar who had been sitting near the temple gate (John 9:1-7). No one else but Jesus would have had any concern for this blind beggar during an escape from the angry Pharisees. But Jesus' heart was so set on His work that even the hateful Jews did not deter Him from His gracious pursuits. Christ Jesus had come into the world to serve and bless men. Jesus had such consideration for others that He was unmindful of Himself. If, while fleeing from His enemies, the Lord stopped to heal a blind beggar, how much more will He bless those who seek after Him now that He is exalted in heaven? The apostle John writes, "As he went along, he saw a man blind from birth" (John 9:1). Many had passed by this poor man and had not seen him at all, and many saw him but were indifferent. The disciples had seen him, but they were not sympathetic; they saw him as a sinner. As far as they were concerned, he was an example of retributive justice; and, therefore, they passed by him with contempt and pride. While Jesus fully admitted to the law of divine retribution, He excluded this case from the category saying, "This happened so that the work of God might be displayed in his life" (v. 3). This man's blindness was for the purpose of illustrating the work that Jesus came to do. Christ came to do these kinds of works of mercy. Jesus said, "We must do the work of him who sent me" (v. 4). Because Jesus was so others-oriented, He could not sit still and see men perish. He could not have come down from heaven and been a passive spectator of so much suffering. Jesus was compelled by the misery around Him. The blind man's condition had touched the Savior's heart. He felt for that blind man. Jesus' hungering and thirsting to do good culminated in the grandest of all acts, the sacrifice of Himself.

"On a Sabbath Jesus was teaching in one of the synagogues, and a woman was there who had been crippled by a spirit for eighteen years. She was bent over and could not straighten up at all" (Luke 13:10-11). On no day of the week was the Lord so closely watched by His adversaries as on the Sabbath. They were hoping to trap Him in some breach of the Mosaic Law. On this particular Sabbath, Jesus was teaching in a synagogue. There Jesus saw a woman who had been afflicted in her body for eighteen years. Lockyer writes:

> For eighteen long years she had endured her deformity, described first of all as "a spirit of infirmity" which does not mean that she was of a weak and infirm spirit. The phrase denotes one of those mysterious derangements of the nervous system, having their rise in the mind rather than in the body. Her physical curvature was the consequence of mental obliquity, making her melancholy. Thus her strange malady was partly physical and partly mental.[61]

The woman's disease had rendered her very short in stature, possibly half her original height; and consequently, like other very short persons, she was almost lost in a standing crowd. Luke says that "Jesus saw her" (v. 12). The gracious eyes of the Lord glanced past all the rest and lighted upon her. Jesus was

---

61 Herbert Lockyer, *All the Miracles of the Bible* (Grand Rapids: Zondervan Publishing House, 1961), p. 223.

always looking for people to serve. Instantly Jesus spoke words of comfort and kindness to her. He called her to Him. Down the aisle she came, pitiful, bent over, and unable to look up. She had not asked Him for healing. Jesus saw her misery and singled her out as a special object of His divine mercy. He laid His hands on her and poured His strength into her, and immediately the woman straightened up and praised God.

On his last journey to Jerusalem, Jesus passed through Jericho. When he had visited Jerusalem a few months before, he had cured a blind man (John 9). Quite possibly, the news of this healing inspired the faith and hope of the blind beggars. As the crowd followed after Jesus, one of the blind men perceived that something unusual was going on and spoke not only for himself but also for his blind companion. He asked what all the commotion was about. He was told that Jesus of Nazareth was passing by on His way to Jerusalem. Blind Bartimaeus had heard of Christ's gracious and wonderful works and believed that Christ was the long-awaited Messiah. When He heard Bartimaeus's cries for mercy, "Jesus stopped" (Mark 10:49). Jesus was always on the move, active, energetic, and doing good works. Full of love and mercy, Jesus had never waited for men to find Him, "for the Son of Man came to seek and to save what was lost" (Luke 19:10). Christ did not loiter around in the streets, but was always on the move for the purpose of doing good to others. Earlier Jesus had told His disciples that they were going to Jerusalem and that He would be betrayed and crucified (Mark 10:33-34). Although Jesus' thoughts were preoccupied with the events that would occur in Jerusalem, He nevertheless stopped. The blind beggar of Jericho had stopped the Savior on His way to the cross. Mark writes that Bartimaeus began to shout, "Jesus, Son of David, have mercy on me" (Mark 10:47). A cry for mercy stopped Jesus in His tracks. Jesus was ready to help. He asked, "What do you want me to do for you?" (v. 51). Jesus often asked questions of those desiring healing. Jesus would ask the needy to express their need and faith in words. The beggars asked for mercy, and at once the Lord showed it: "Jesus had compassion on them" and healed them.

About a month before His own death and resurrection, Jesus raised Lazarus from the dead (John 11:1-44). When the news had reached Jesus that His dear friend Lazarus was sick, He sent words of comfort to Mary, Martha, and Lazarus: "This sickness will not end in death" (John 11:4). Jesus, who was others-oriented, taught His disciples to be others-oriented; He continued, "No, it is for God's glory so that God's Son may be glorified through it." Mary and Martha were sure that Jesus would come, but "he stayed where he was two more days" (v. 6). Lazarus was encouraged because he had heard that his sickness would not end in death, but then Lazarus died. Weeping and wondering why Jesus had not come, Lazarus' sisters were sitting by his corpse. Mary and Martha asked themselves how Jesus' words could have been true when their brother lay dead. It must have been painful for the Lord to bring grief to Mary and Martha by allowing Lazarus to die. Strangely enough, Jesus told His disciples that He was "glad" that He was not there to have prevented Lazarus' death. Jesus said, "And for your sake I am glad I was not there, so that you may believe" (v. 14). Christ was not glad because of their grief, but because He knew that temporary trial would increase their faith. In other words, Christ said, "I am glad for your sakes I was not there to prevent the tragedy, because since it has come, it will teach you to believe in me, and that is much better than if you had been spared the sorrow." Herein lies a great principle: the Lord in His infinite wisdom and love places such a high value on His people's faith that He does not shield them from those trials and difficulties by which their faith is strengthened.

But Christ, our sympathetic High Priest (Hebrews 4:14), did not deal with His people in a cold and mechanical way. Jesus' heart was touched by their infirmities and weaknesses. Jesus wept when He thought of Lazarus and his weeping sisters. In all their grief, Jesus was grieved, and so He wept. Jesus stood face to face with the last enemy—death. He saw what sin and the devil had done to mankind. Jesus' whole person was stirred, and His love made Him weep. As Jesus moved past the crowd and toward the grave of His friend, Jesus' tears flowed and caused the bystanders to say, "See how he loved him!" (v. 36). The heart of Christ that had found expression for Mary and Martha's sorrow in tears also reached out to help them. Christian sympathy should be like Christ's sympathy, which was not content with words and tears, but led to practical compassion. When Jesus thought about man's terrible condition, in which sin reigns and rules over him and man has become subject to death, He wept. But greater still was Jesus' act of love in dying on the cross. Jesus had to pour out His life, not only His tears that men might see how deeply He loves.

The healings and miracles of the Lord Jesus Christ abundantly prove both His compassion and His power to save. Jesus was others-oriented. He sympathized with all sufferers. Though sometimes Jesus had no time to eat or rest, He always found time to heal bodily diseases. Jesus healed others not hurriedly, as if He were bothered, but lovingly, as an essential part of His mission. Jesus healed diseases because He was the Conqueror of sin, and He constantly pointed out that sickness and death resulted from sin. There was no kind of suffering which Jesus did not relieve. Those that were regarded as unclean were welcomed, and those whom none could cure Christ healed. Like the heavenly Father, of whom Jesus was the "Image," He was kind to the unthankful and unworthy. Christ Jesus condescended to be wrapped in swaddling clothes and laid in a manger. He Who created all things and upholds all things was Himself weary and hungry. The miracles of Jesus Christ reveal that faith in Him was the supreme virtue and that the paramount goal in life was to increase one's faith, not to have self-esteem. Unlike Josh McDowell who claims that "A healthy sense of self-worth is fundamental in drawing us closer to God,"[62] Jesus

---

62 Josh McDowell, *Building Your Self-Image* (Wheaton: Tyndale House, 1978), p. 47.

taught and modeled that faith was basic and necessary. Time and time again the Lord praised men for their faith or scolded them for their lack of faith. The apostle Paul writes, "The just shall live by faith" (Romans 1:17). The Lord never asked anyone about his self-image. Jesus never inquired, "How do you feel about yourself?" Christ's concern was, "Who do people say that the Son of Man is?" (Matthew 16:13). Mark told us that blind Bartimaeus shouted "Jesus, Son of David, have mercy on me" (Mark 10:47). His confession of faith that Jesus was the Son of David, the Messiah, moved Jesus to heal him. While the selfists praise men for their self-love, Jesus was "astonished" by the centurion's great faith. As vital as self-love is said to be to a healthy life, and as much "pain" as the lack of it is said to cause, one would think many would have sought Jesus for "emotional healing." But there is no record of any who came to Him and cried, "I hate myself, I feel inferior and inadequate; heal me Son of David." Jesus' focus was always on the person's faith. Christ's concern for a person's faith was founded in His concern for the person's fellowship with Him. The Lord wanted each person to trust Him and in doing so He healed him.

Chapter Four

The Parables of Jesus Christ

Jesus' emphasis on the others-oriented way of life and its incompatibility with the self-oriented way of living is also seen in Jesus' parables. Indeed, the parabolic method itself displays Jesus' others-oriented character. Jesus had used parables before, but the parable of the Sower was the first full parable He used. There came a time when definite and active hostility toward Jesus' claims became apparent to all. Mark explains, "He looked around at them in anger . . . deeply distressed at their stubborn hearts" (3:5). The rulers had "hardened" hearts, which in turn stirred up the crowds. A stubborn or hardened heart was characterized by callousness, blindness, and determination not to listen or obey. When the rulers did listen to Jesus, they did so for the purpose of criticizing and being destructive. At that time Jesus began speaking to the multitudes in parables. When the Lord became angry over the hardness of their hearts, He expanded His use of parables. His anger was the result of His love and grace (others-oriented), in spite of their attitudes. Jesus said, "In them is fulfilled the prophecy of Isaiah: 'You will ever be hearing but never understanding; you will be ever seeing but never perceiving'" (Matthew 13:14). Why? "For this people's heart has become calloused . . . ." (v. 15). The Savior was grieved by the hardness of their hearts. That was one reason He used the parabolic method. When the disciples asked why Jesus used parables, He gave a second reason—so that they could know the mysteries of the kingdom of God. To His disciples, who were obedient and submitted to Him, the mysteries were made known. From other people, who were disobedient and rebellious and had hardened hearts, the mysteries were hidden in parables. Jesus compared His parables to a shining lamp (Mark 4:21-25) that illuminated hidden things. These people did not see or hear the mysteries of the kingdom because of their attitudes. Christ's disciples had received the mysteries of the kingdom, but to those outside the kingdom the parable was like a lamp. G. Campbell Morgan explains:

> He gave them parabolic pictures, so that they might inquire. The purpose of the story, the picture, was to lure them to think, in order that they might find their way into the higher mystery. Our Lord did not intend then to use the parable to prevent men seeing, that would also contradict the whole purpose of God in Christ, but to help them to see. He did not want to prevent them from hearing, but to quicken their power of hearing. He did not keep men away from the forgiveness and mercy of God, but He lured them towards it.[63]

Chapter thirteen of Matthew contains eight parables that reveal Jesus' view of the kingdom of heaven. These parables view the kingdom in its historical sense when Christ came into the world, in its progress in this age among men. The kingdom of God and man's redemption and transformation into that kingdom are the subject from the beginning to the end. This therefore also demonstrates that the Lord was others-oriented.

For example, in the two short parables of the Hidden Treasure and the Pearl Merchant, Christ's kingdom is represented as being a hidden treasure. The field is the world (13:38). The good seed is the Son of Man (13:37). Here is a picture of the world and Christ's relationship to it. The man found a treasure in the field. He purchased the field and hid the treasure. The treasure, which represents the kingdom, was revealed and rejected by the nation of Israel. The consequence was that Christ rejected Israel. Matthew writes, "Therefore I tell you that the kingdom of God will be taken away from you and given to a people who will produce its fruit" (21:43). A full manifestation of the kingdom was postponed to a future age when Christ would come in His glory the second time.

---

63 G. Campbell Morgan, *The Parables and Metaphors of Our Lord* (New York: Fleming H. Revell, n.d.), p. 17.

Christ then turned to a larger work illustrated by a man's selling all that he had to purchase a field. We see in this parable the complete revelation of the work of Jesus Christ. It is expressed in the words: "And then in his joy he went and sold all he had and bought that field" (Matthew 13:44). In other words, Jesus emptied Himself. Jesus sold all He had to buy the field (the world) to redeem lost men. The only way to possess the field was through self-denial. Paul writes, "For you know the grace of our Lord Jesus Christ, that though He was rich, yet for our sakes he became poor, so that you through His poverty might become rich" (2 Corinthians 8:9).

To have spiritualized these parables would not change their others-oriented focus. For example, in the parables of the Hidden Treasure and the Pearl Merchant, the kingdom is represented as being hidden, and yet it was the supreme find to those who discovered it (Matthew 13:44-46). The parable of the Hidden Treasure is about a man who was suddenly and unexpectedly brought face to face with eternal life in Jesus Christ. This man was going about his life, earning a living and raising a family. Suddenly, circumstances that seemed purely accidental occurred and he heard the gospel of the kingdom of God. We do not know how this man's eyes were opened to the Lord. There are many ways that the providential hand of God stirs a man's heart and gets him thinking about his soul. In this case the parable shows us that there may be a finding without any previous seeking. The point is the man knew the value of what he had discovered, so he earnestly sold all to acquire it. Likewise, the pearl merchant was earnest to possess what he had discovered; but unlike the other man, his discovery was the result of an intentional search for the true meaning and purpose of life. The man set out with steadfast perseverance. The pearl was discovered. The pearl was the Lord Jesus Christ Himself. Both men were others-oriented. The one sold all that he had to buy the field, while the other sold all that he had to buy the pearl. Both men's minds were aroused and engaged in obtaining what they had found. All their energies, thoughts, and finances were fixed upon a definite object: The kingdom of heaven. Those who spiritualize the parable of the Pearl Merchant say that it is a picture of the sinner seeking Christ.

The parable of the Lamp on a Stand (Mark 4:21-25; Luke 8:16-18) and the parable of the Growing Seed (Mark 4:26-29) will be considered together. The lesson we again learn from these parables is that Christians, like their Savior, ought to be others-oriented. Christians should do good to others; in other words, they should bring forth fruit. Our Lord asked the question, "Do you bring in a lamp to put it under a bowl or a bed? Instead, don't you put it on its stand?" (Mark 4:20). The apostles were meant to receive the gospel, not for themselves only, but for the good of others, to communicate it to them. Putting a lamp under a bed would be to hide it from others (self-oriented), but placing the lamp on its stand would be to help others. Though Christ expounded the parables to His disciples privately, His design was to make the disciples more publicly useful. They were taught by the Lord for the purpose of teaching others. The apostle Paul writes, "Now to each one the manifestation of the Spirit is given for the common good" (1 Corinthians 12:7), not for himself only, but for others. The sower was others-oriented, for he was laboring in God's "field" and scattering the Word liberally to all types of men. The sower's only responsibility was to put the seed into the soil of men's hearts. The sower's work was indispensable. The parable also denotes the necessity of God's divine influence. There had to be both divine and human agency, for the parable said that after sowing "night and day, whether he sleeps or gets up, the seed sprouts and grows, though he does not know how" (v. 27). For example, Paul had planted the seed, Apollos had watered it, "but God made it grow" (1 Corinthians 3:6). The sower was not able to hurry the growth. Jesus said that the sower *had* to sleep and rise day and night. The Lord's doings were invisible and incomprehensible and were a great encouragement to both the faith and patience of the sower who waited upon the Lord to bring the harvest. Both faith and patience, which are the main features of this parable, are others-oriented virtues that Christ taught and modeled.

At one point, while speaking to a crowd, Jesus was interrupted by a listener who presented a most inappropriate demand: "Teacher, tell my brother to divide the inheritance with me" (Luke 12:13-21). R. C. Trench writes, "It was the extreme inopportuneness of the season for urging his claim, that showed him as one in whom the worldly prevailed to the danger of exclusion of the spiritual."[64] In other words, the man was self-oriented (worldly), as opposed to others-oriented or God-oriented. The Lord refused to intercede in the matter because it was outside the sphere of His proper mission. "Jesus replied, 'Man, who appointed me a judge or an arbiter between you?'" (v. 14). He warned the man against the sin of covetousness and indicated that "A man's life does not consist in the abundance if his possessions" (v. 15b). To teach him the lesson, Jesus related a parable about a certain right man whose concern was to multiply his possessions, but who was surprised by death while doing so. This rich fool had left all of his wealth behind and entered into eternity poor. A great mistake men often make is that they think they can satisfy the desires of their hearts by gaining wealth. All the effort to be satisfied with things or gifts, when the Giver is left out, proves to be vain. No abundance of anything can satisfy the craving heart of men.

Jesus skillfully portrayed the egotism of the rich fool. When we examine the man's words, we find six "I's" and four "my's." This parable applied to both of the brothers quarreling over the inheritance. Both were selfish. One brother had hoarded the inheritance and would not give his brother his portion, while the other coveted his brother's riches. So Jesus again warned them both against the sin of covetousness: "This is how it will be with anyone who stores up things for himself but is not rich toward God" (v. 21). He contrasted self-orientation and others-orientation with the words "himself" and "God." Again Trench says, "Self and God are here contemplated as the two poles between which the soul is placed."[65] The man who lays

---

64 R. C. Trench, *Notes on the Parables of Our Lord* (Grand Rapids: Baker Book House, 1990), p. 117.
65 *Ibid*, p. 119.

up treasures for himself continually squanders on worldly objects those affections which he ought to give to God.

The Christian self-theorist would agree that the rich man in the parable is guilty of pride. However, using theological acrobatics, the Christian self-love theorist claims that self-love is not the same as negative, unhealthy, or sinful pride but is positive, healthy, constructive pride, or self-esteem. For example, Schuller writes:

> And if my pride as a person is rooted in my relationship as a son of the Almighty, then my pride is purged of arrogance and takes the noble face of self-dignity and honor! Do not fear pride; the easiest job God has is to humble us. God's almost impossible task is to keep us believing every hour of every day how great we are as his sons and daughters on this planet.[66]

Self-esteem theology redefines and dulls men's consciences in regard to sin. The offensiveness of sin to God is minimized. Schuller claims that the core of sin is a "negative self-image, but do not say that the central core of the human soul is wickedness. If this were so, then truly, the human being is totally depraved."[67] So, not only has self-esteem theology redefined sin, but it also has redefined salvation. Again Schuller provides us with an example, saying, "To be born again means that we must be changed from a negative to a positive self-image—from inferiority to self-esteem."[68]

The prominent idea in the parables of the Wedding Feast and the Wise Servant is that of preparedness for Christ's coming (Luke 12:35-48). All the members of the household of faith were to be found serving each other and laboring together as unto their King (others-oriented). In the parable of the Rich Fool Jesus had already warned against covetousness, to which

---

66 Robert Schuller, *Self-Esteem: The New Reformation* (Waco: Word Publishing, 1982), p. 57.
67 *Ibid.*, p. 67.
68 *Ibid.*, p. 68.

rich people, who trust in the abundance of their riches, were most susceptible. The disciples, who were poor men, thought that they were immune to this sin, but Christ warned them against another kind of covetousness which they were most tempted to commit. Jesus said to them, "Do not worry about your life, what you will eat; or about your body, what you will wear" (v. 22). He warned them about being covetous, which would lead to anxiety over the necessary supports of life such as food and clothing. Jesus encouraged the disciples to have faith and presented the common sense argument that if God provided for the lesser things that He had created such as the birds and the lilies of the field, He would provide for them. Jesus taught them that an inordinate pursuit of the things of this world, even necessary things, characterized pagans. Pagans were self-oriented and sought after these things. Christians, who should be others-oriented, must ask and trust their heavenly Father for these things. The disciples' focus was to be on God and His kingdom, and the lesser things God would provide (v. 31). Then Christ gave His disciples the parables. Jesus charged them to "Be dressed ready for service . . . like men waiting for their master to return from a wedding banquet." The disciples' concentration was to be on serving Christ and waiting for His coming.

The parable of the Barren Fig Tree (Luke 13:6-9) was told to enforce Christ's words of warning, "But unless you repent, you too will all perish" (v. 5). The parable is a picture of Almighty God in His gracious dealings with men. The parable introduces a proprietor of a vineyard. As the owner he had certain rights. The vineyard, soil, and fig tree belonged to him. There was an obligation on the part of the fig tree to provide fruit for the owner. In this parable we learn of the punitive right of the proprietor to destroy the tree which fails to produce fruit. The parable focuses on the proprietor, God. God's rights are the absolute rights of proprietorship. God planted the vineyard. The tree existed for the owner. In the same way, we exist to glorify our heavenly Father (others-oriented).

The parable of the Barren Fig Tree teaches that God's patience is enjoyed by many who hear the gospel yet do not bring forth the fruits of the gospel, provoking God to wrath. This was not the first time that the vinedresser had been aware of the fig tree's barrenness. Neither was this the first time that the owner had come and found it barren. So, the owner said, "Cut it down!" The vinedresser interceded for the fig tree and pleaded to the owner of the vineyard: "Sir, leave it alone for one more year . . . ." In this same way Christ is the great Intercessor who asks for time for His people. Christ ever lives; His sparing mercy causes Him to intercede for others. Just as fruit is the product of the tree's life and the reason for the tree's existence, so too obedience to God's will is the product of a man's life. For that reason man was created. When a man plants a tree, he expects it to provide him with fruit. The tree exists for the one that planted and cared for it. Naturally, those who are God's property, who are created for Him, and who are objects of His providential care, should glorify Him by their lives. They should be God-oriented (others-oriented) and not self-oriented.

In the parable of the Two Builders, Christ taught the importance of obeying His word as well as hearing His word (Matthew 7:24-27; Luke 6:47-49). These were the closing words of the Savior's now famous Sermon on the Mount. Jesus simply and affectionately gave a warning to those who, having heard His words, would have remained satisfied with hearing and would not have put them into practice. Obedience to Christ, Who is the Rock, was the foundation upon which the wise man was said to have built. The wise man's success was not in himself or in the materials he used to build, but in the foundation on which he built. The wise builder was others-oriented, and he recognized the necessity of a firm foundation. His house stood firmly in the storm, while the foolish man's house, built upon a sandy foundation, fell down. The only sure foundation for men's souls and eternity, according to the parable, is to hear and obey the words of the Lord Jesus Christ.

The parable of the Unmerciful Servant illustrates the matter of forgiveness—not God's forgiveness of man, but man's forgiveness of man (Matthew 18:21-35). This parable was the Lord's reply to Peter's question regarding the frequency of forgiveness. Peter asked, "Lord, how many times shall I forgive my brother when he sins against me? Up to seven times?" Jesus' answer stunned Peter, "Seventy times seven." The parable consisted of a contrast of attitudes and activities about debt. A man owed his master a great amount of money which he was not able to repay. The man's master ordered him and his family to be sold and payment to be made. The man fell down before him and begged for his master's mercy. The master realized the poverty-stricken condition of the debtor. Moved with compassion, he wiped out the entire debt. The master had dealt with his servant in a most compassionate way, but the servant, in turn, dealt harshly and unmercifully with a fellow servant who owed him a much smaller debt. The master, having learned of the violent, ungrateful attitude of his forgiven servant, was angered and so delivered him up to jailers to be punished. The lesson is that one ought to behave toward others as God behaves toward him. Notice how the compassion of God, Who is others-oriented, shines behind the scenes of this wonderful parable. God grants forgiveness, not because of any worth in man, but because He is merciful.

The Good Samaritan is a picture of true benevolence and selflessness (Luke 10:25-37). Jesus used the parable to answer two questions asked by a lawyer, "an expert in the law." The first question was, "What must I do to inherit eternal life?" (v. 25). The Lord answered that with a question, "What is written in the law?" (v. 26). The lawyer answered, "Love the Lord your God with all your heart and with all your soul and with all your strength and with all your mind, and love your neighbor as yourself." Then the lawyer asked the second question, "And who is my neighbor?" (v. 29). Luke tells us that the lawyer said this to justify himself. He was not trying to justify himself to the crowd that was standing around, but he was trying to justify his own conscience. Then the Lord told the parable. The Samaritan had no relationship with the Jew; he was a foreigner. Yet he pitied his unfortunate Jewish neighbor. The Samaritan came by, and immediately his heart was touched, "he had compassion on him." In the New Testament, *compassion* is always used to describe Jesus, and no one else, except as Jesus used it in this case. Compassion is the motivator for keeping the law of God. Compassion is others-oriented. What did compassion inspire the Samaritan to do? It inspired him to perform personal service to the wounded man. The Samaritan bound up the injured man's wounds and poured oil and wine on them. Then the Samaritan lifted the man onto his donkey, carried him to town, and made provision for him. The Samaritan did not hesitate; he did what was needed for the injured man. He thereby proved to be a neighbor. Neighborliness required self-surrender. The final word of the parable calls for responsible action: "Go and do likewise."

The fundamental principle of the Christian ethic, love of God and neighbor, is illustrated by this beloved parable of the Good Samaritan. Jesus commended the lawyer for answering correctly, "Love the Lord your God with all your heart and with all your soul and with all your mind. This is the first and greatest commandment. And the second is like it: Love your neighbor as yourself" (Matthew 22:37-39). Love was the priority and was no longer just one in a series of requirements demanded by the Torah; it was "greater" than all the others (see also Matthew 22:37-40; Mark 12:29-31). Love is others-oriented. Christians who have propagated self-love have made a feeble attempt to turn this passage upside-down and have said that the phrase "as yourself" exhorts one to recognize one's self-worth. However, Jay Adams writes:

> Christ made it perfectly clear that He was talking about two, and only two, commandments. In verses 39 and 40 He speaks of the "second" commandment and "these two commandments." There is no third commandment. All of

> Scripture can be hung on two pegs: Love God,
> Love neighbor. Yet the self-esteem people make
> three commandments out of Christ's two! There
> is absolutely no excuse for treating the Scriptures
> in this manner. As if distortion of plain scriptural
> teaching were not enough, they go further and
> make the first two commandments depend upon
> the supposed "third." [69]

The text does not urge a self-love, but a selfless love of others.
The love described here is directed outward to the other, not
inward toward the self. Jesus said, "Which of these three do
you think was a neighbor?" (Luke 10:36). The neighbor, not
self, is Christ's focus in the passage. The essence of sin is man's
preference for self instead of God. Instead of making God the
center of his life, instead of surrendering himself in subordination
to God's will, the sinner makes himself the center and sets
himself up against God. Therefore, man would love God more
than himself, were sin not present.

The parable of the Great Supper was told in the house
of one of the rulers of the Pharisees (Luke 14:15-24). The Lord
and a man suffering from dropsy had been invited to supper on
the Sabbath. This act of hospitality had a sinister motive. Jesus
was being "carefully watched" to see if He would heal the man
on the Sabbath. Jesus healed the man, then criticized the guests
for their bad manners and the host for the false pretense on
which he had given the invitation. Jesus spoke about a marriage
feast and a dinner. He taught two principles of hospitality and
social order. First, Jesus said that self-emptying was the true
secret to exaltation (vv. 7-11). Then, turning to the host, Jesus
demonstrated that self-emptying was the secret of hospitality.
Jesus said, "When you give a luncheon or dinner, do not invite
your friends . . . if you do, they may invite you back and so you
will be repaid" (v. 12). The key word was "if." Generally people
invite people to be invited back by them, to be repaid. At that

---

69 Jay Adams, *The Biblical View of Self-Esteem, Self-Love, Self-Image* (Eugene: Harvest House, 1986), p. 67.

moment someone said, "Blessed is the man who will eat at the feast in the kingdom of God" (v 15).

At this point, Jesus told the parable of a man who prepared a great supper and invited many guests. The guests all made excuses and declined the invitation to partake of the feast (self-oriented). The man extended another invitation to the poor, crippled, and blind. The first call represents salvation offered to the Jews, and their rejection of the Savior. The second call to the poor, crippled, and blind represents salvation offered to the Gentiles who had welcomed the Savior and eagerly entered the kingdom. The third call was to an even lower class, the homeless, and tramps who lived on the streets. Those who accepted the hospitality are described as blessed or happy. Those that entered in, entered only by grace. What a diverse crowd are those who, down through the ages, God has called to salvation. The redeemed come from all walks of life. Millions of them, who were spiritually corrupt, impaired, and impoverished, have accepted the royal invitation.

Usually, the parables found in Luke 15 have been broken up by writers and preachers, as if they were three distinct parables. The Lost Sheep (vv. 1-7), the Lost Coin (vv. 8-10), and the Lost Son (vv. 11-32) are actually one parable represented by three pictures. Each of the three pictures declares the same main truth, but each reveals a different phase of it. Concern over something lost and joy at the recovery of it are the prominent notes of each part of the parable. Jesus had told the parable of the Great Supper in the house of the Pharisee (14:15-24). Chapter 15 begins with Luke's description of the circumstances: "Now the tax collectors and sinners were all gathering around to hear him. But the Pharisees and the teachers of the law muttered, 'This man welcomes sinners and eats with them'" (vv. 1-2). By means of this threefold parable, Jesus set forth the supreme fact that as the Son of Man He came into the world to seek and to save the lost. "We might have named the three stories of this chapter, 'The Parables of the Four Verbs—Lose, Seek, Find,

Rejoice.'"[70] The criticism, "This man welcomes sinners and eats with them," supplies us with the reason for the parable. In it we see the attitude and activity of God in His gracious (others-oriented) mission to humanity. He received sinners; He did not stand aloof, but He went so far as to sit down and eat with them.

In each part of the parable some object (representing man) is depicted as lost. First, a sheep was lost. The shepherd sought his lost sheep as if it had been the only one he possessed. In this story, divine grace is magnified and the Pharisees were rebuked. Second, the coin was lost. The woman felt the loss of her coin as if it were the only money she owned. Reminding her that she still had nine other coins was of no comfort to her. Finally, a son was lost. The father was brokenhearted over the loss of his younger son. Reminding him that he had another son was not enough. The emphasis of the parable was on the one lost, not on the condition of the thing lost. The emphasis was on the agony of the one who had suffered a loss. The shepherd was suffering more than the wandering sheep. The woman was suffering because of the lost coin. The father was the one who had known the depth of agony when his son had left home. In all these metaphorical stories, man is the true object of divine mercy.

The parable of the Unjust Judge, in Luke 18, is about a widow who sought justice against her adversary. She had appealed for justice to a judge who was supposed to be there to administer it. The judge was described as a man "who neither feared God nor cared about men." For some time the judge refused to help the woman, but she kept coming to him with her appeals for justice. Finally, the judge took action and did what the woman wanted; he meted out justice. He acted because the woman kept bothering him. The judge said within himself, "Even though I don't fear God or care about men, yet because this widow keeps bothering me, I will see that she gets justice, so that she won't

---

70 Herbert Lockyer, *All the Parables of the Bible* (Grand Rapids: Zondervan Publishing House, 1963), p. 283.

eventually wear me out with her coming" (vv. 4-5). The judge was self-oriented. All he cared for was himself; he did not want to be troubled.

Those who propagate self-love would agree that the judge was self-centered, but they would also insist that self-love and self-centeredness are not the same thing. Bruce Narramore writes, "Every infant goes through a stage when he loves only himself. As far as he is concerned, he is the center of the world. Everyone caters to his needs . . . . Unfortunately, some people never outgrow this stage."[71] According to this view, sinful self-centeredness is a result of one's immaturity. Narramore says that self-love that is narcissistic and childish is not "mature self-love" and is not the sort of self-love he advocates. In fact, "It is a sad symptom of a lack of self-esteem."[72] In other words, self-esteem is the cure for self-centeredness. Schuller agrees: "The haughty or arrogant person is really suffering from a tragic lack of healthy self-love . . . . In reality, narcissism is not authentic self-love, but a symptom of a pitiful lack of it."[73] Self-theorists, in an attempt to integrate self-love with the others-oriented nature of the Scriptures, insist that sinful pride, self-centeredness, are not the same as healthy or authentic pride, self-love. This distinction, which was never taught or modeled by the Lord, is necessary to the selfist in light of the biblical teachings on the sinfulness of pride and selfishness. To the layman, it would seem that men are selfish and narcissistic because they are self-oriented and love themselves, but self-esteem advocates have said that the exact opposite is true. They claim that the congruity between self-love and narcissism is only apparent. To the selfist, men are selfish because they don't love themselves enough and are benevolent when they do.

Our Lord's purpose in presenting this parable was not (as many believe) to teach that we must persist in prayer until God, like the unjust judge, grudgingly gives in. In fact, the opposite

71 Bruce Narramore, *You're Someone Special* (Grand Rapids: Zondervan Publishing House, 1978), p. 36.
72 *Ibid.*, p. 37.
73 Robert Schuller, *Self-Love* (New York: Jove Books, 1969), pp. 25, 26.

is true. The main point of the parable is to contrast the judge's attitude and actions with God's. God is not unjust and selfish. God cares for man. The judge was indifferent to the widow's case. When the judge finally took action, he did so in order to escape personal suffering and annoyance. But notice what Jesus said about God: "And will not God bring about justice for his chosen ones, who cry out to him day and night?" (Luke 18:7). If they go to God, He will not delay. Although God's actions cost Him, God will act on His people's behalf. The judge's action was self-motivated. God's action is motivated by His willingness to suffer all things for us. God is always listening, and His people do not need to keep on as though God were reluctant to exercise justice. In other words, there is no need to try to persuade God to do what is right and good.

Like the previous parable, the parable of the Pharisee and the Sinner is about the subject of prayer (Luke 18:9-14). Its purpose is revealed in Jesus' telling it "to some who were confident of their own righteousness and looked down on everybody else." Jesus addressed a particular attitude some held about themselves: that of being righteous while looking down on others. Two men went into the temple to pray. But there was a difference between these men. Though the Pharisee went up to the temple to pray, he did not truly pray at all. In contrast to the Pharisee was the Publican (or sinner). True humility was the one virtue that the Publican had. He went up to the temple to pray and said, "God, have mercy on me, a sinner" (v. 13). This was true, unadulterated prayer. The Pharisee's prayer was full of pride and self-conceit and self-congratulation. It was also a prayer conspicuous for its four big I's. The Pharisee's words moved in a circle and paraded his merits in the presence of God. The center and circumference of his prayer was self. The sinner's prayer was full of humility and self-loathing. One boasted of his righteousness, while the other confessed and repented of his sin. Both stood in need of mercy. The Pharisee "stood up" and prayed. He took his stand apart from the sinner, in the forefront of the temple at the usual hour of prayer. The sinner, because he was not the kind of man that usually came to pray and mingle with the regular worshipers, stood alone just inside the doorway of such a holy place. He had crept in and stood at a distance from the altar; the place where he stood was central to his conception of God. "He would not even look up to heaven, but beat his breast and said, 'God have mercy on me, a sinner.'"

In contrast to the biblical account given here, Schuller says, "No matter what has happened in your life you are not . . . 'a hopeless sinner.' After twenty years in the field of people-counseling I have heard that exaggerated, distorted, destructive lie repeated many hundreds of times."[74] One lesson we can learn from the sinner's confession is that one of the foundations of godly character is a personal sense of sin. Sin results in a separation from God, and to confess sin, to be penitent, is not morbid or "unhealthy." Man is by nature an enemy of God, in bondage to sin, and a lover of himself. Yet man is relentlessly proud. The sinner in the parable was timid and humble; his only thought was about his sinfulness. He prayed alone because he considered himself unworthy. When he beat his chest and prayed, "God have mercy on me, a sinner," he did so because he had a true self-image. He saw himself for what he was, and this view led to self-condemnation, repentance, and forgiveness. Therefore, Jesus said, "This man, rather than the other, went home justified before God" (v. 14). Jesus commended rather than rebuked the sinner for his low self-esteem.

In the parable of the Two Sons, and the parable of the Wicked Tenants, Jesus condemned the religious leaders who had gathered round about Him (Matthew 21:28-46). The Pharisees challenged Jesus' authority saying, "By what authority are you doing these things? . . . And who gave you this authority?" The key to both parables is found in the words, "When the chief priests and the Pharisees heard Jesus' parables, they knew he was talking about them" (v. 45). The Pharisees had felt the power of His truth; in their answers to Jesus' interspersed questions, they pled guilty, chose their own punishment, beheld His mercy, and plotted His death.

---

74 Robert Schuller, *Self-Love* (New York: Jove Books, 1969), pp. 25, 26.

In the parable of the Two Sons, the father commanded his sons to go and work in his vineyard. The son who said, "I will not," but afterwards changed his mind and went, represents penitent sinners such as the tax collectors and harlots. They lived in open sin and made no profession of obedience. They knew they were sinners. Under the preaching of John the Baptist, these people, who were rebellious and defiant toward God, repented and became sons of God and went to work in His vineyard (others-oriented). The son who said, "I will sir," but did not go, was a picture of the Pharisees. Professing to be the Lord's, they were disobedient and recalcitrant. While they were outwardly correct and righteous, they were inwardly wretched and, in the end, rebellious (self-oriented). Both sons were sinful and false. Their different answers only indicated different sins. The first son was arrogant and guilty of open sin. The second son was deceptive. The one son had not promised or intended to obey. The other son promised and did not intend to obey. Only in their ultimate act were they different. The first son changed from rebellious to obedient and was others-oriented. The second son did not change, and remained self-oriented.

But Jesus was not finished. He continued by telling the parable of the Wicked Tenants. The Pharisees had discounted Him as the Son of God, rejecting His authority. Jesus, in a further condemnatory parable, set forth who He was and the death He was to die at their hands. There was a proprietor of a vineyard who sent his servants to gather up fruit from his vineyard, but the tenants stoned the servants and killed them. Then the proprietor sent others, with the same result. Finally Jesus said, "He sent his son to them" (v. 37; what tremendous force there must have been in those words). "But when the tenants saw the son, they said to each other, 'This is the heir. Come, let's kill him'" (v. 38). After the story, Jesus pressed the Pharisees for their judgment about the tenants. Their verdict was immediate and was really a judgment upon themselves. The Pharisees replied, "He will bring these wretches to a wretched end, and he will rent the vineyard to other tenants" (v. 41).

The Faithful and Wise Servant, The Ten Virgins, and The Talents are related parables, all referring to the consummation of the age (Matthew 24:45-25:30). Chapters 24 and 25 constitute one body of thought in the teaching of our Lord, occasioned by a prediction that He made about the destruction of the Temple and the question then raised by the disciples as a result of that prediction. All three parables speak of an absent lord and his impending return. None of the master's servants knew for certain when he would come; therefore, they had to be prepared and be watching. A threefold responsibility is revealed in the three parables. There is a *communal* responsibility depicted in the parable of the Faithful and Wise Servant regarding the way in which God's people should behave toward one another in His absence. In the parable of the Ten Virgins, there is the *individual's* responsibility to be watchful and prepared for the Lord's return. Finally, in the parable of the Talents, there is a *kingdom* responsibility. Goods had been entrusted to God's people, and while He was away, they were to be used for His purposes.

The parable of the Faithful and Wise Servant begins with the question, "Who then is the faithful and wise servant whom the master has put in charge of the servants of his household?" (Matthew 24:45). This parable reveals the responsibility of those who were watching. What was their responsibility? Jesus said that when He comes He wants to find His servant busy "doing." Doing what? Giving the servants whom God has put him in charge of "their food at the proper time." The servant who had been put in charge of the household was to rule and care for those under him. He was to unite, inspire, lead them to be subject to their master, and feed them with the Truth (others-oriented).

In the parable of the Ten Virgins, the Lord was once again referring to the consummation of the age. He continued the solemn declaration of the uncertainty of the time of His return and the duty on the part of His servants to be prepared for His coming. The emphasis of this parable was on the servant's life rather than on his work as he anticipated the coming of the Lord (others-oriented). Everything culminated in that final word of Jesus' in the thirteenth verse: "Therefore, keep watch, because you do not know the day or hour."

The emphasis of the parable of the Faithful and Wise Servant is on faithful service to others. The parable of the Ten Virgins emphasizes watchfulness. The parable of the Talents focuses on one's duty to work for the Lord. R. C. Trench explains, "While the virgins were represented as waiting for their Lord, we have here the servants working for Him."[75] Looking for Christ's return, Christians should labor in light of it. "Again, it will be like a man going on a journey, who called his servants and entrusted his property to them" (Matthew 25:14). The picture here is of a man who went on a journey, left his servants to whom he had distributed his wealth (talents), and directed them to trade for him, to carry out his business in his absence. The master called them his servants. The emphasis was on his authority and possession. All the talents belonged to the master and were handed over to his servants to be used for the glory and enrichment of their absent lord. Two of the servants were others-oriented. They focused on being wise investors for their lord and were congratulated by their lord for their faithfulness. "It says of those two servants that they came to their lord upon His return and said, 'Master, you have entrusted me with five/two talents. See, I have gained five/two more'" (vv. 20, 22). Their focus was on increasing their master's wealth. The third servant was self-oriented and failed to trade and multiply the master's talents. His excuse was that he feared his master, who might punish him if he lost his talents: "Master, I knew you were a hard man . . . so I was afraid" (vv. 24-25). The truth about him is revealed by Jesus' words: "You wicked and lazy [self-oriented] servant."

The account of the Feet-Washing is a parable by way of example, "Jesus knew that the time had come for him to leave

---

75 R. C. Trench, *Notes on the Parables of Our Lord* (Grand Rapids: Baker Book House, 1990), p. 91.

this world and go to the Father. Having loved his own who were in the world, he now showed them the full extent of his love" (John 13:1). Jesus loved His disciples. He loved them and pitied them when He saw them lost, like sheep without a shepherd, and then He called them out of the world to be His own. Jesus was touched by their infirmities and ignorance, and with tenderness, patience, and affection He trained and educated His disciples in God's ways. Even when Jesus had rebuked them for their self-centeredness just moments before He washed their feet, He loved them with an everlasting love. The disciples had experienced many trials and hardships. Sharing His cross daily, they were persecuted as they accompanied our Lord from town to town. But His love for them reigned supremely, never diminished, in spite of all their selfishness, desertions, denials, and frailties. Spurgeon writes:

> He had selected persons who must have been but poor companions . . . He must have been greatly shocked at their worldliness . . . . He was thinking of the baptism wherewith he was to be baptized . . . but they were disputing which among them should be the greatest. He was ready to deny himself that he might do the Father's will, and meanwhile they were asking to sit on his right hand and on his left hand in the kingdom. Earthworms are miserable company for angels, moles but unhappy company for eagles, yet love made our great Master endure the society of his ignorant and carnal followers.[76]

Jesus was always faithful toward His chosen ones. This is another way Jesus was others-oriented.

The disciples were only thinking about their own pre-eminence in the kingdom of heaven: "A dispute arose among them as to which of them was considered to be greatest" (Luke 22:24). At this point, we can see the significance of what Jesus

---

76 Charles H. Spurgeon, *The Metropolitan Tabernacle Pulpit*, vol. 3 (Pasadena: Pilgrim Publications, 1976), p. 266.

did when he washed the disciples' feet, for He was obviously not giving just an example of humility. Jesus was giving a dramatic illustration of His entire ministry. He showed the disciples what He came into the world to do and what He would send them out to do. To enforce this truth, Jesus illustrated it by taking the place of a slave, whose duty was to wash the feet of those who entered the house. Such an act was beyond Peter's comprehension, so at first he objected to it. Later in his life Peter came to understand, and he then declared the symbolic significance of his Lord's self-emptying action when he wrote, "Young men, in the same way be submissive to those who are older. All of you, clothe yourselves with humility toward one another, because, 'God opposes the proud, but gives grace to the humble'" (1 Peter 5:5). Jesus carried the basin of water and knelt in the attitude of a slave. God's grace was exquisitely depicted as Jesus knelt before His disciples. What a marvelous scene to behold as Christ emptied Himself, humbled Himself, bent over in order to perform the most menial of tasks, the work of a slave. Truly this act is a wonderful revelation of God's grace. These divine rules of self-sacrifice and esteeming others were the rules that governed the Lord Jesus Christ. The disciples would have thwarted His selflessness, for they were astonished and unsubmissive when He girded himself and knelt at their feet. Neither Peter nor any of the disciples showed a pinch of humility, as was evidenced in their competitiveness and dispute over who was greatest. The disciples esteemed themselves, so they reasoned: should not their Master, who was greater than they, esteem Himself above them? How unthinkable to them that Jesus should have denied Himself and engaged in such menial activity!

Jesus then told the disciples the significance of His actions. He showed the importance of observing in daily life the principles that undergirded those actions. Jesus reminded the disciples of the way they addressed Him, as teacher. This term expresses the very great reverence they had toward Jesus. He commended the disciples, for this expression pointed to His true position. This exalted Person esteemed His disciples above

Himself and had washed their feet. They then were to esteem one another above themselves and should have washed one another's feet.

Chapter Five
Conclusion

Our study of the life of Jesus clearly shows that the Lord Jesus Christ was others-oriented and not self-oriented. A general analysis of Jesus' words, miracles, and parables demonstrates that Jesus consistently taught and modeled that one should focus on God and neighbor, and not on oneself (Matthew 22:37-40).

For example, as a child Jesus' deepest concern was to be obedient to His parents (Luke 2:41-52). He never tried to usurp their authority over Him. He humbled Himself to be baptized by John the Baptist in order to fulfill the Scriptures (Matthew 3:13-17). Jesus denied Himself and was tempted by the devil in the wilderness of Judea in order to become a sympathetic High Priest (Matthew 4:1-11). In the Sermon on the Mount, Christ commanded that an offended or offensive brother "go" and initiate biblical reconciliation (Matthew 5:21-24). Jesus instructed people to love their enemies (Matthew 5:39-48). He told believers to seek first the kingdom and righteousness of God (Matthew 6:33). Later, Jesus told the twelve apostles that all of His followers must deny themselves and take up their cross (Matthew 10:1-39). At other times, He spoke of selling all or of losing one's life (Matthew 10:39). On another occasion, Jesus said that the greatest commandment was to love God and that the second greatest commandment was to love one's neighbor (Matthew 22:37-40). In the Garden of Gethsemane, Jesus focused on God's will and not His own (Matthew 26:39), thus giving a model for believers to follow. Finally, as the Lord was crucified, He prayed for His murderers and not for Himself (Luke 23:34).

Jesus' miracles also illustrate His others-oriented way of living. The miracles of Christ mirror His character and express His love and sympathy for suffering mankind. The Lord's loving selflessness is suggested in Luke's description of this Miracle-

Worker as One who went about doing good (Acts 10:38). For example, in Capernaum the Lord healed the nobleman's son who was near death (John 4:43-54). On a mountainside in Galilee Jesus healed a man with leprosy (Matthew 8:1-4). He also raised the widow's son in a small town called Nain (Luke 7:11-17). Near Bethsaida, the Lord fed five thousand hungry people (Matthew 14:13-21). On the road to Jericho, Christ gave sight to a blind man named Bartimaeus (Matthew 20:29-34).

Jesus' parables further display His others-oriented way of living. The conspicuous feature of Christ's parables is their portrait of Christ's selfless character and work. His grace and mercy toward sinful men is seen in the parable of the Debtors (Luke 7:40-50). The Lord's patience is depicted in the parables of the Lost Sheep and Growing Seed (Luke 15:3-7; Mark 4:26-29). His compassion for those who are suffering is seen in the parable of the Good Samaritan (Luke 10:30-37). The parable of the Prodigal Son pictures Christ's selfless love for sinners (Luke 15:11-32). His tenderness and pity are demonstrated in the parable of the Lost Sheep (Luke 15:1-7). Jesus' care is the prominent feature in the parables of the True Vine and the Good Shepherd (John 15:1-8; John 10:1-30).

People already love themselves. For that reason Jesus carefully warned His followers of the dangers of pride and self-love. Jesus repeatedly emphasized the fact that self is the problem and that self-denial is the pathway to true godliness. In coming into the world to do the Father's will, Jesus' concern for others was so intense that He "forgot Himself." The Lord did His work so wholeheartedly that He was not even aware of Himself. Even when His work for the day was done, Jesus retreated into solitude where He became "lost" in communion with God the Father.

Before the Fall, Adam and Eve were others-oriented; their focus was on God and each other; self was never an issue. All of the evil, wickedness, and ruin that came from sin resulted in man's turning from doing God's will to doing his own will. As Isaiah 53:6 says, "We all, like sheep, have gone astray, each of us has turned to his *own* way" (italics mine). Ever since the intrusion of sin into the world, man has been self-oriented. Selfism became the natural disposition of man's sinful heart: "Self has usurped the throne, a usurper who never abdicates. Self is the new and false center upon which man has fixed. He loves himself as nothing else under the sun. Even his best deeds are but refined form, the filthy rags, of his secret selfishness."[77] The object of the redemption in Christ Jesus is to restore man *to do God's will.* For this Jesus died. He gave up His own life rather than do His own will. Jesus died according to the Father's will to redeem man. Christ was others-oriented.

Nothing was more striking in Christ's earthly life than His others-oriented attitude of absolute submission to the Father: "Here I am, I have come to do your will" (Hebrews 10:9). That perfectly encapsulates Jesus'earthly life and ministry. Jesus came, as He said, not to do His own will, not to speak His own words, not to seek His own glory, not to teach His own doctrines. Jesus repeatedly emphasized His entire submission to the Father in redeeming fallen humanity by His denial of self. Scripture tells that Jesus set His face toward Jerusalem to die. He marched into the enemies' camp, so to speak. Jesus knew what would happen when He got to Jerusalem, yet He went. Jesus was either being foolish or going for a sublime purpose. Why did He go to Jerusalem? What did Jesus say? "Just as the Son of Man did not come to be served, but to serve, and to give his life as a ransom for many" (Matthew 20:28). "This is my blood of the covenant, which is poured out for many for the forgiveness of sins" (Matthew 26:28). "I am the good shepherd. The good shepherd lays down his life for the sheep" (John 10:11). The Savior looked upon His death as the necessary condition for man to have forgiveness from sin and reconciliation to God. Jesus' humiliation was vicarious and substitutive in nature. He never focused on self but on God and neighbor.

Self was never an issue or a motivating factor for the Lord. He said, "I am among you as one who serves" (Luke 22:27). Obedience to God and service to others were the

---

77 L. E. Maxwell, *Born Crucified* (Chicago: Moody Press, 1973), p. 56.

motives that guided Him. Jesus did not speak like the selfist, who claims people must urgently seek to love themselves. Jesus never showed any concern about people having too little self-esteem; therefore, He gave no instructions on how one should enhance self-esteem. Jesus taught selflessness, and modeled it by becoming subordinate, pleasing and honoring God the Father. Jesus' words, depicting His relationship to His Father, demonstrate how unceasingly He used the words *not* and *nothing* when describing Himself. "The Son can do *nothing* by himself" (John 5:19). "By myself I can do *nothing*; I judge only as I hear, and my judgment is just, for I seek *not* to please myself but him who sent me" (John 5:30). "I do *not* accept praise from men" (John 5:41). "For I have come down from heaven *not* to do my will but to do the will of him who sent me" (John 6:38). "My teaching is *not* my own. It comes from him who sent me" (John 7:16). "I am *not* here on my own" (John 7:28). "I am *not* seeking glory for myself" (John 8:50). These words reveal the deepest thoughts of Christ's life and works. Jesus communicated that He was nothing, in order that God the Father might be everything.

However, the selfist would diagnose anyone speaking as the Lord spoke to be suffering from an inferiority complex, possibly traceable to traumatic early childhood experiences. In other words, Jesus' feelings of inadequacy and incompetency were due to the "ill treatment" He was subjected to by Mary and Joseph. According to Josh McDowell, "The initial development of our self-image lies in our relationships with our parents. A child literally discovers what kind of person he is and how he feels about himself by the reactions of his parents to him."[78] The consensus of self-theorists can be summed up by the title of Dr. Susan Forward's book, *Toxic Parents: Overcoming Their Hurtful Legacy and Reclaiming Your Life*. Of course, the *Christian* self-theorist, after learning that it was Jesus who spoke the words of self-denial in the previous paragraph, would deny that evaluation. The Christian self-theorist's explanation would be

---

78 Josh McDowell, *Building Your Self-Image* (Wheaton: Tyndale House, 1984), p. 70.

that Jesus' selflessness was the product of His perfect self-love. As a pastor friend of mine once said, "Jesus was self-actualized." Jesus' self-image was not lopsided, unstable, or shaky. He loved Himself perfectly; therefore He loved others. This conclusion is consistent with the presuppositions of humanistic psychology, but not with the words and actions of the Lord. Jesus never said or insinuated that His compassion and love for others was due to His perfect self-love.

When Christ was on the earth, He continually brought people face to face with the impossible. His commands were contrary and unreasonable to self. How impossible and unreasonable it was for Jesus to command His followers to love their enemies, pray for those who persecuted them, and rejoice in suffering. These behaviors are against human nature—in other words, against man's self-will. Jesus' purpose was to bring man face to face with man's self-oriented will and God's others-oriented will, man's self-oriented ways and God's others-oriented ways. The Savior was shaking man at his foundation, his self-orientation. For example, Christ blessed the poor in spirit, the meek, and those that mourn. Jesus contradicted what was "natural," and demonstrated that God's thoughts and ways are not man's thoughts and ways (Isaiah 55:8, 9). Jesus' intent was to bring man's focus and will into submission to His. This was why Christ talked about His own cross. In His words, miracles, and parables, Jesus taught and modeled the principle of the cross.

The cross was a perfect contradiction of everything that Jesus' followers thought was sensible, right, and good. The cross was *the* expression of Jesus' own perfect obedience and willful submission to His Father. The principle of the cross, which is denying of self, emptying of self, and being others-oriented, was seen in Christ's condescension and humiliation: "Who is like the Lord our God, the One who sits enthroned on high, who stoops down to look on the heavens and the earth?" (Psalm 113:5, 6). All that He did, all notice that He gave to even the most glorious of His creatures, was an act of infinite condescension. There was a vast distance between Jesus' essence, nature, and being and the essence and nature of man. Therefore, He said, "Surely the nations are like a drop in a bucket; they are regarded as dust on the scales . . . all the nations are as nothing . . . worthless and less than nothing" (Isaiah 40:15, 17). That He took notice of things below was an act of mere grace. How glorious was the condescension of the Son of God, in His assumption of the office of Mediator and Priest. A priest is a man duly appointed to act for other men in things pertaining to God. The idea which lies at the foundation of the office of priest is the idea that men, being sinners, do not have access to God. Therefore, the one who has that right in himself, or the one to whom that right has been conceded, must be appointed to draw near to God on behalf of sinners. By the nature of his office, a priest is a mediator, and he is thus others-oriented. The priest's function is to reconcile men to God, to make expiation for their sins. The New Testament gives an authoritative definition of the word *priest*: "Every high priest is selected from among men and is appointed to represent them in matters related to God, to offer gifts and sacrifices for sins" (Hebrews 5:1). Not only is Christ called a priest in Hebrews, but the apostle also throughout that epistle proves that Christ Jesus had all the qualifications for the office.

The apostle Paul writes, "Your attitude should be the same as that of Christ Jesus: Who, being in very nature God . . . made himself nothing, taking the very nature of a servant, being made in human likeness . . . he humbled himself and became obedient to death—even death on the cross!" (Philippians 2:5-8). Christ's attitude was what the apostle commanded men to imitate. Christ's attitude, the opposite of autonomy (self-rule) and self-orientation, was one of subjection to God's rule, which is the principle of the self-emptying or no-self (kenosis). Jesus' intent was to bring His disciples through the terrible process of inner crucifixion of their own self-wills and into submission to God. "Then Jesus said to his disciples, 'If anyone would come after me, he must deny himself and take up his cross and follow me'" (Matthew 16:24). Cross-bearing was a commonly used figure of speech in Christ's day. It stood for doing a thing that was disagreeable and painful. Cross-bearing involved crucifixion of self and the sacrifice of one's natural feelings and inclinations. Jesus made clear beyond any shadow of doubt that the "must" of self-denial applied to His disciples no less than to Himself. Discipleship meant adherence to the person of Jesus and, therefore, submission to the way of Christ, which is the way of the cross. Discipleship was others-oriented.

Jesus also offered Himself as teacher. Jesus said, "Take my yoke upon you and learn from me, for I am gentle and humble in heart, and you will find rest for your souls" (Matthew 11:29). Unlike Fromm, Maslow, Adler, Rogers, Peale, Dobson, Schuller, Narramore, Crabb, etc., Christ made all things plain, simple, and clear. Plainness and simplicity are hardly characteristic of any of the writings of Christian or secular self-theorists. Humanistic explanations of man that attempt to suppress God's Word, by denying it totally or denying it through integration of their humanism with the Scriptures, are forever complex, and nonsensical. The self-theorist always has an explanation. But his explanation only leads to more questions and longer and more complicated explanations—hence the multiplication of theories and the lack of consensus. The self-theorist builds his edifice higher and higher. When he builds himself into the proverbial corner, he just knocks a hole in the wall, makes a new door for himself, and keeps on building. However, "God is not a God of disorder but of peace" (1 Corinthians 14:33).

Meekness and lowliness, not self-love, were the things Jesus taught His disciples, because the disciples were always esteeming themselves. For example, the love of self was strong in Peter. Peter had left his boats and his nets, but he was still self-oriented in his attitudes and thoughts. When Christ spoke to him about His cross, Peter rebuked His lord. But Jesus then said to Peter, "Get behind me Satan! . . . . You do not have in mind the things of God [others-oriented], but the things of men [self-oriented]." Jesus followed those words with, "If anyone would come after me, he must deny himself and take up his cross and follow me" (Mark 8:34). To learn from Jesus meant to follow

Him. The strangeness of the command "follow Me" was central to the gospel. Jesus did not lead men to esteem themselves—that was the devil's work. The devil was full of self-esteem (Isaiah 14:13-14). The devil encouraged Eve to be autonomous and esteem herself above God: "For God knows when you eat of it your eyes will be opened, and you will be like God" (Genesis 3:5). To follow Christ, self must be denied. What does that mean? When Peter denied Christ, he said three times: "I don't know him" (Luke 22:57). In other words, Peter had nothing to do with Jesus. Peter denied being Jesus' friend or companion, to protect himself. But Christ told Peter he must deny self. Self must be ignored and its every claim rejected. That is the root of true discipleship.

Today, however, self is not denied. Self is exalted, pampered, and esteemed. The words of Christ have been reversed. Self-love is deemed a necessary pre-requisite to discipleship, sanctification, and understanding what being a Christian is really about. The authors of *Christian Self-Esteem: Parenting by Grace* write:

> As we help children grow in self-esteem, we teach them what it means to be a Christian. We prepare them for a maturing faith which will give them meaning and hope when we cannot be there to cheer them on . . . the healthier a child's self-esteem, the greater is their belief in God. One of your most important ministries as a Christian parent is the shaping and nurturing of your child's self-esteem.[79]

Christ used the word *deny* twice with Peter—the first time, "deny himself" (Matthew 16:24), the second time, "thou shalt deny me" (Matthew 26:34 KJV). There was no other choice for Christ's disciples; they would either deny self (others-oriented) or deny Christ (self-oriented). To deny oneself means self is not significant. Only Jesus matters. Jesus is esteemed.

---

79 Diane Garland, Kathryn Chapman, and Jerry Pounds, *Christian Self-Esteem: Parenting by Grace* (Nashville: Lifeway Press, 1991), pp. 22, 24.

The Christian selfist sees the cross and proudly proclaims, "I am significant, special, worthy, and highly esteemed." In contrast, when Isaiah saw the Lord, he trembled and said, "Woe to me! . . . . I am ruined! For I am a man of unclean lips, and I live among a people of unclean lips" (Isaiah 6:5). While the selfist glories in himself, the apostle Paul writes, "May I never boast except in the cross of our Lord Jesus Christ, through which the world has been crucified to me, and I to the world" (Galatians 6:14). The author of Hebrews writes, "Let us fix our eyes on Jesus [not on self] the author and perfecter of our faith, who for the joy set before him endured the cross" (12:2). The cross was supreme in the ministry, purpose, and thoughts of the Redeemer, and it must be supreme in Christians' lives as well. Self-sacrifice is their calling. To the Christians who have been taken captive by the hollow and deceptive philosophy of self-love, the cross is a means to covet and boast in self. To the truly spiritual person, however, the cross is the power of God that unhinges and tears man loose from his foul and false self-infatuation. F. J. Huegel writes:

> How strange the Cross of Christ makes inroads into our "self-life" with the force of a terrible army bent on utter destruction. Yet we cannot resist its attractive force. We greatly err when we conclude that the forgiven sinner who has now found a place in the kingdom of God's Holy Son, is done with the cross. In a sense he has just begun. The Cross of Christ is now to become his home, his life, his all in all.[80]

The Heavenly Father's will is that each of His children, beginning with Christ the first-born, practice self-denial by taking up his cross (Matthew 16:24). Christians are not exempt from the condition to which Christ their Head had to submit, especially since He submitted to it for their sake to show them an example. The apostle Paul taught that God has destined all His children

---

80 F. J. Huegel, *The Cross of Christ—The Throne of God* (Grand Rapids: Zondervan Publishing House, 1956), p. 64.

to the end that they be "conformed to the likeness of his Son" (Romans 8:29).

Jesus said, "And glory has come to me through them" (John 17:10). The Lord was praying for His immediate followers. Jesus gave several reasons why He was praying for His followers. One reason was their calling in life, described in John 17:10. Jesus reminded His followers of their function and business in the world. Jesus told them that His Father had sent Him into the world, and now He was sending His followers into the world (v. 18). When God sent His Son into the world, He had a specific objective in mind. His Son was to do certain things, and the greatest of all was to glorify His Father in heaven. The Lord Jesus said that He sent His followers into the world for a reason exactly parallel to that for which God had sent Him, to glorify Him. The sequence and the context of this amazing statement is full of significance. First, the Lord said in this prayer that He glorified the Father. Second, Jesus revealed that the Holy Spirit had been sent to glorify the Son. This is abundantly clear in the chapters leading up to chapter 17. The phrase "After Jesus said this" (John 17:1) refers to chapters 14, 15, and 16, containing the great teachings about the Holy Spirit. These teachings are summed up by Jesus' words: "He will bring glory to me" (16:14). The Holy Spirit comes and enters the believer, and the believer glorifies the Son. Glorifying the Son (others-oriented) is the focus and work of the Christian. Believers are brought into this sequence of giving glory that involves the blessed Holy Trinity. All is for the glory of God. The Son came: He lived and died. Everything Jesus did was others-oriented. The Holy Spirit came and glorified the Son. The Holy Spirit was others-oriented. The Christian, as the result of the operation of the Holy Spirit, also is to glorify the Lord Jesus Christ. The believer is to be others-oriented. Peter writes in his first epistle, "But you are a chosen people, a royal priesthood, a holy nation, a people belonging to God, that you may declare the praises of him who called you out of darkness into his wonderful light" (2:9). The apostle Paul says God's purpose in redeeming His people is "the praise of his glorious grace which he has freely given us in the One he loves" (Ephesians 1:6). Calvin writes:

> The duty of believers is "to present their bodies to God as a living sacrifice, holy and acceptable to him" (Romans 12:1). From this is derived the basis of the exhortation that "they be not conformed to the fashion of this world, but be transformed by the renewal of their minds, so that they may prove what is the will of God" (Romans 12:2). Now the great thing is this: we are consecrated and dedicated to God in order that we may thereafter think, speak, meditate, and do, nothing except for his glory. For a sacred thing may not be applied to profane uses without marked injury to him . . . . We are not our own: let us therefore not set it as our goal to seek what is expedient for us according to the flesh . . . . We seek not the things that are ours but those which are of the Lord's will and will serve to advance his glory . . . . For he who has learned to look to God in all things that he must do, at the same time avoids all vain thoughts. This, then, is that denial of self which Christ enjoins with such great earnestness upon his disciples at the outset of their service (Matthew 16:24).[81]

The self-esteem movement in the church has its roots in humanistic psychology. The Personality theories of clinical psychologists such as Alfred Adler, Erich Fromm, Abraham Maslow, and Carl Rogers have only recently been incorporated into the teachings of the church. Though this incorporation has been relatively recent, the self-esteem movement began early in human history. It started back in the third chapter of the Book of Genesis.

---

81 John Calvin, *Institutes Of the Christian Religion*, vol. 20 (Philadelphia: Westminster Press, n.d.), pp. 690, 691.

In the beginning, Adam and Eve were others-oriented. They focused on God and neighbor. Their self-awareness or self-consciousness was incidental to their focus on God and one another. Self was not an issue. Then the great tragedy of man's fall from a state of innocence and fellowship with God to his present state of sinfulness and alienation gave birth to the emphasis on self. Therefore, mankind sought and continues to seek fulfillment and gratification through an unnatural focus on self. In one sinful act, man became self-oriented.

The crucifixion of the Lord Jesus Christ was the crowning sin of man's self-orientation. At the same time, it was Christ's crowning example of self-forgetfulness. There on the cross Christ was "made a curse for *us*," He "bore *our* sins," God "laid on him the iniquity of *us* all," He was "made to be sin for *us*," He "took up *our* infirmities and carried *our* sorrows," He was "pierced for *our* transgressions . . . crushed for *our* iniquities," and He "tasted death for *every* man." A Christian who esteems himself is a contradiction in terms. To be a Christian is to be like Christ. Christ esteemed others and denied Himself.

If evangelicals are to be evangelicals they must no longer compromise their view of Scripture. This is the only way to be faithful to what the Bible teaches about itself and what Christ taught about Scripture. The apostle Paul writes, "I want you to know brothers that the gospel I preach is not something that man made up. I did not receive it from any man, nor was I taught it; rather I received it by revelation from Jesus Christ" (Galatians 1:11, 12). Notice his emphasis on the word *revelation*. The Bible is infallible and sufficient because it is from God. It is truth from heaven, not from men. This has always been the orthodox evangelical position. This strong view of Scripture, with its absolutes, is the main line of defense against subjective-relativistic thinking that has led to selfism and other heresies. Unfortunately, many who claim to be evangelicals are not united for a strong view of Scripture. Only a strong view of Scripture will lead to a Godward focus and an allegiance to a Christian worldview. This worldview will be characterized by a theocentric (God-centered) perspective on all of life and thought. The theology which has become more and more humanistic-anthropocentric (man-centered) exalts man and is the essence of sinfulness. Sin is not just the absence of love for God, defined in purely negative terms; rather, it is also a positive preference for self as the object of one's affection. Instead of being others-oriented with God at the center, the sinner is self-oriented and places himself at the center. We must lovingly but clearly draw the line between those who take a full view of Scripture and those who do not. In addition, we must lovingly instruct believers who profess an orthodox view of the Scriptures but who do not understand that selfism-theology is unorthodox.

Christians must learn to accurately evaluate, or "think soberly," about themselves: "Do not think of yourself more highly than you ought, but rather think of yourself with sober judgment, in accordance with the measure of faith God has given you" (Romans 12:3). Paul goes on to talk about the different gifts and responsibilities that God gives to each member of His church. Self-evaluation must be made in the context of the exercising of one's gifts. Therefore, "sober judgment" refers to judgment based on actions or behavior. In contrast, selfists insist that all individuals should "judge" themselves highly, merely because they are human and have been made in the image of God.

A sober evaluation must be made by comparing one's actions to biblical standards, not by comparing oneself to *others*. For example, in the parable of the Pharisee and the Sinner, the Pharisee's boast was that he was not like other men, especially like the sinner who stood at the rear of the temple. Another example is Paul's instructions to the Galatians. These believers, in their attempt to restore a fallen brother, held a false opinion of themselves by thinking they were not as easily tempted as their fallen brother. Paul warned them, saying, "If anyone thinks he is something when he is nothing, he deceives himself" (Galatians 6:3).

A man cannot exercise "sober judgment" by self-reflection. In other words, a man cannot ask himself how he is doing and evaluate his actions by *himself*. Once again, he must evaluate his behavior by biblical standards. Sin has made man's thinking "futile," his heart has become "darkened," and his claim of being "wise" is inaccurate. Man's self-analysis is flawed by sin (see Romans 1:21-22). God's Word must always correct man's image of himself: "For my thoughts are not your thoughts, neither are your ways my ways, declares the Lord" (Isaiah 55:8). The principle is this: sinful human thought opposes God's thought and perverts biblical values and standards. When man attempts to evaluate himself, he has a tendency to overestimate, rather than underestimate. Only God can correctly evaluate man's behavior.

The self-theorist teaches that as human beings, men have the right to feel good about themselves and should seek to love themselves, regardless of how they behave. However, Christians should not focus on self or on pursuing self-worth. Believers are to be others-oriented and are commanded to "live [behavior] a life worthy of the calling [they] have received" (Ephesians 4:1). The Savior never instructed His disciples to esteem themselves, but to deny themselves. In the parable of the Talents, the Lord said, "Well done, good and faithful servant! . . . . Come and share your master's happiness!" (Matthew 25:21, 23). The believer's satisfaction, joy, and peace come as by-products of faithful and fruitful Christian living.

Every heresy in the history of Christ's church has dishonored God and flattered man. The one purpose, openly or covertly, has been to exalt man and rob God of the glory due to Him. On the other hand, the true gospel always brings man low and lifts God high upon His throne. In effect, then, this gives a test to distinguish heresy from the true gospel, whereby even a babe in Christ is able to discover counterfeit teachings, even if he is not yet able to refute them. The test is simple. Does the teaching glorify God? If it does, it is true. Does it glorify man? If it does, it is not true. Does is depreciate man or appreciate man? Does it put a crown upon God's head or man's head?

Only the Lord Jesus Christ can esteem Himself. He alone has the right to do so. Consider Christ's eternal existence. The prophet Micah says that although the Savior will be born in Bethlehem, He existed previously "from everlasting" (5:2 KJV). John begins his gospel by writing, "In the beginning was the Word." Jesus Christ was in the beginning, before the world was created (John 1:1). On the island of Patmos John describes Jesus as "the Alpha and the Omega, the First and the Last, the Beginning and the End" (Revelation 22:13). With Christ Jesus there is no distinction between the past, present, and future. Jesus is and always has been and always will be.

Consider next Christ's omniscience. Matthew states that Jesus knew the thoughts of the Pharisees (12:25). John says that "he knew all men" (2:24). His disciples said to Him, "Now we can see that you know all things" (John 16:30). Jesus had no limitations or imperfections in His knowledge. No one had to tell Him anything. He was infinitely perfect in His understanding. The writer of Hebrews declares, "Neither is there any creature that is not manifest in his sight: but all things are naked and opened unto the eyes of him with whom we have to do" (4:13 KJV).

Christ may also justifiably esteem himself because of His omnipresence. In Matthew 28:20 the Lord said, "I am with you always, to the very end of the age." There are no limitations on Christ Jesus; therefore, He fills all with His presence. He is equally with all of His creatures all of the time in all places. A man may confidently say, "The Lord is in this place."

Jesus is also omnipotent, for He said, "all power is given unto me in heaven and in earth" (Matthew 28:18 KJV). He demonstrated that He had the power to forgive sin, raise the dead, heal the sick, cast out demons, walk on water, calm the winds, give up His life, and take His life back again—He could do whatever He willed. Mere humans must use means to accomplish their ends. With Jesus, means are not necessary. Jesus wills, and it is done. As the Psalmist writes, "Our God is in heaven; he does whatever pleases him" (Psalm 115:3). His power is absolute and free from all restraints; He carries out His plans unthwarted by men.

All of these attributes are the essence of deity. Jesus Christ is God and, therefore, has every right to esteem Himself above others. Jesus said to His disciples, who realized His superiority to them, "You call Me 'Teacher' and 'Lord', and rightly so, for that is what I am . . . no servant is greater than his master . . . ." (John 13:13-16). When the Lord went to John the Baptist to be baptized, John's reply exhibited his understanding of Jesus' superiority to him: "I need to be baptized by you" (Matthew 3:14). Jesus did not reject John's statement and acknowledgment that He was indeed greater than him. Jesus knew He alone was worthy; nevertheless, He washed His disciples' feet and submitted to John's baptism, again showing His humility and others-orientation. Scripture does not say He was humbled, but that He humbled Himself. The willingness of His humility made it acceptable to His Father. Paul writes of Christ's deity: He was "in very nature God" (Philippians 2:6). Christ Jesus was the same in substance with God the Father before the world was created. The Savior could have focused on His own glory, and it would have been entirely appropriate. Man's heart tells him he is worthy, but his heart lies to him. Only Christ is significant and worthy. While on earth Christ never ceased to be God, nor was His Godhead separated from His humanity; He was always glorious (James 2:1). He was the radiance and brightness of the Father's splendor (Hebrews 1:3), but His glory was veiled and clouded so that He did not look like Himself. He appeared to be just a man—"being found in appearance as a man" (Philippians 2:8)—but He was more. His magnificence is seen in the fact that He concealed His glory. He was God, "but made himself nothing, taking the very nature of a servant, being made in human likeness" (Philippians 2:7). For the Lord Jesus Christ to take upon Himself the nature even of an angel would have been a great stoop, but, behold, He assumed the nature of sinful men for the purpose of doing them good.

As mere humans, we must be careful not to presume that we can unravel all the mysteries of God with our carnal minds. Some things are too wonderful. There are certain aspects of the works of God, like Christ's humiliation, that we can never fathom. Our Lord's self-abasement is like a great ocean, and we are like little children, oblivious to the great depths, playing in the waves that wash up on the beach. The apostle Paul proclaims of these things, "Oh, the depth of the riches of the wisdom and knowledge of God! How unsearchable his judgments, and his paths beyond tracing out! Who has known the mind of the Lord? Or who has been his counselor?" (Romans 11:33, 34). However, we do know by what Jesus said and modeled that the impulse to serve lies at the very heart of God. God is not self-oriented, but others-oriented. Christ Jesus did not esteem Himself. He did not look upon His own interests, but the interests of others. "Your attitude should be the same as that of Christ Jesus" (Philippians 2:5).

Bibliography

Adams, Jay E. *The Biblical View of Self-Esteem, Self-Love, and Self-Image*. Eugene: Harvest House, 1986.

Adams, Jay E. *The Christian Counselor's Manual*. Grand Rapids: Zondervan Publishing House, 1973.

Adams, Jay E. *Competent to Counsel*. Grand Rapids: Zondervan Publishing House, 1970.

Adams, Jay E. *From Forgiven to Forgiving*. Amityville: Calvary Press, 1994.

Adams, Jay E. *Theology of Christian Counseling*. Grand Rapids: Zondervan Publishing House, 1979.

Bancroft, Emery. *Christian Theology*. Grand Rapids: Academie Books, 1961.

Bobgan, Martin and Deidre Bobgan. *Prophets of Psychoheresy I*. Santa Barbara: Eastgate Publishers, 1988.

Bobgan, Martin and Deidre Bobgan. *Prophets of Psychoheresy II*. Santa Barbara: Eastgate Publishers, 1990.

Bonhoeffer, Dietrich. *The Cost of Discipleship*. New York: Macmillan, 1961.

Branden, Nathaniel. *Honoring the Self*. New York: Bantam Books, 1985.

Branden, Nathaniel. *The Psychology of Self-Esteem*. New York: Bantam Books, 1985.

Bridges, Jerry. *The Practice of Godliness*. Colorado Springs: Navpress, 1983.

Brownback, Paul. *The Danger of Self-Love*. Chicago: Moody Press, 1982.

Bruce, Alexander Balmain. *The Training of the Twelve*. Cincinnati: Jennings and Graham, n.d.

Bruce, F.F. *The New International Commentary on the New Testament*. Grand Rapids: William B. Eerdmans, 1971.

Buckley, Ed. *Why Christians Can't Trust Psychology*. Eugene: Harvest House, 1993.

Calvin, John. *Commentary*, vol. 16. Grand Rapids: Baker Book House, 1981.

Calvin, John. *Institutes of the Christian Religion*, vols. 1, 20. Philadelphia: Westminster Press, n.d.

Cole, Donald. *Basic Christian Faith*. Westchester: Crossway Books, 1985.

Crabb, Larry. *Basic Principles of Biblical Counseling*. Grand Rapids: Zondervan Publishing House, 1975.

Crabb, Larry. *Effective Biblical Counseling*. Grand Rapids: Zondervan Publishing House, 1977.

Crabb, Larry. *Inside Out*. Colorado Springs: Navpress, 1988.

Crabb, Larry. *Understanding People*. Grand Rapids: Zondervan Publishing House, 1987.

Dobson, James. *Dr. Dobson Answers Your Questions*. Wheaton: Tyndale House, 1982.

Dobson, James. *Hide and Seek*. Grand Rapids: Fleming H. Revell, 1974.

Flavel, John. *The Works of John Flavel*, vol. 1. New York: Banner of Truth, n.d.

Forward, Susan. *Toxic Parents*. New York: Bantam Books, 1990.

Fosdick, Harry Emerson. *On Being a Real Person*. New York: Harper & Brothers, 1943.

Fromm, Erich. *The Art of Loving*. New York: Bantam Books, 1956

Fromm, Erich. *Man for Himself*. New York: Holt, Rinehart and Winston, 1961.

Garland, Diane, Kathryn Chapman, and Jerry Pounds. *Parenting by Grace: Christian Self-Esteem*.　　　Nashville: LifeWay Press, 1991.

Hall, Calvin, and Lindzey Gardner. *Theories of Personality*. New York: Wiley & Sons, 1957.

Harris, Thomas. *I'm OK—You're OK*. New York: Avon Books, 1969.

Haas, Guenther H. *Major Themes in the Ethics of John Calvin*. St Louis: Covenant Theological Seminary,   1985.

Henry Matthew. *Commentary*, vol. 5. Old Tappan: Fleming H. Revell, n.d.

Hodge, Charles. *Systematic Theology*. Grand Rapids: Baker Book House, 1988.

Huegel, F.J. *The Cross of Christ—The Throne of God*. Grand Rapids: Zondervan Publishing House, 1956.

Hoekema, Anthony. *The Christian Looks at Himself*. Grand Rapids: William B. Eerdmans., n.d.

Kempis, Thomas. *Of the Imitation of Christ*. Philadelphia: David McKay Company, n.d.

Lloyd-Jones, Martyn. *Fellowship with God*. Wheaton: Crossway Books, 1982.

Lloyd-Jones, Martyn. *Knowing the Times*. Carlisle: Banner of Truth, 1989.

Lloyd-Jones, Martyn. *Studies in The Sermon on The Mount*. Grand Rapids: Zondervan Publishing House,   1978.

Lockyer, Herbert. *All the Miracles of the Bible*. Grand Rapids: Zondervan Publishing House, 1965.

Lockyer, Herbert. *All the Parables of the Bible*. Grand Rapids: Zondervan Publishing House, 1978.

Lohse, Eduard. *Theological Ethics of the New Testament*. Stuttgart, Germany: Augsburg Fortress, 1991.

MacArthur, John Jr. *Biblical Counseling*. Dallas: Word Publishers, 1994.

Maclaren, Alexander. *A Garland of Gladness*. Grand Rapids: William B. Eerdmans, 1945.

Maslow, Abraham. *Motivation and Personality*. New York: Harper & Rowe, 1954.

Maslow, Abraham. *Toward a Psychology of Being*. New York: Insight Books, 1962.

Matson, T.B. *Biblical Ethics*. Cleveland: World Publishing Company, 1967.

Maxwell. L.E. *Born Crucified*. Chicago: Moody Press, 1973.

McConkey, James. *The Surrendered Life*. Pittsburgh: Silver Society, 1903.

McDowell, Josh. *Building Your Self-Image*. Wheaton: Tyndale House, 1978.

McGee, Robert. *Search for Significance*. Nashville: LifeWay, 1992.

Morgan, G. Campbell. *The Gospel According to Matthew*, vol. 6. New York: Fleming H. Revell, n.d.

Morris, Leon. *The New International Commentary on the New Testament: The Gospel of John*. Grand Rapids: William B. Eerdmans, 1981.

Murray, Andrew. *Absolute Surrender*. Springdale: Whitaker House, 1982.

Murray, Andrew. *Freedom from a Self-Centered Life: Dying to Self*, Minneapolis: Bethany House, 1977.

Murray, Andrew. *God's Best Secrets*. Grand Rapids: Zondervan Publishing House, 1917.

Murray, Andrew. *Humility*. Fort Washington: Christian Literature Crusade, 1980.

Narramore, Bruce. *You're Someone Special*. Grand Rapids: Zondervan Publishing House, 1978.

Nichols, James. Ed. *Puritan Sermons 1659-1689*. Wheaton: Richard Owne Roberts Publishers, 1981.

Owen, John, *The Glory of Christ*. Chicago: Moody Press, 1949.

Peale, Normal. *The Power of Positive Thinking*. New York: Fawcett Crest, 1992.

Pink, Arthur. *An Exposition of the Sermon on the Mount*. Swengel: Bible Truth Depot, 1950.

Poole, Matthew. *Poole's Commentary*, vol. 3. Mclean: MacDonald Publications, n.d.

Rogers, Carl. *On Becoming a Person*. Boston: Haughton Mifflin, 1961.

Ryle, J.C. *Expository Thoughts on the Gospels*, vol. 3. Grand Rapids: Zondervan Publishing House, 1951.

Schuller, Robert. *Self-Esteem: The New Reformation*. Waco: Word Publishers, 1982.

Schuller, Robert. *Self-Love*. New York: Jove Books. 1978.

Schaeffer, Francis. *A Christian World View of the Bible as Truth*. Westchester: Crossway Books. 1982.

Spurgeon, Charles H. *The Metropolitan Tabernacle*, Pulpit, vols. 3, 31, 52. Pasadena: Pilgrim   Publications, 1980.

Spurgeon, Charles H. *A Treasury of Spurgeon on the Life and Works of Our Lord*, vols. 4, 6. Grand Rapids: Baker Book House, 1979.

Trench, RC. *Notes on the Miracles of Our Lord*. Grand Rapids: Zondervan Publishing House, 1987.

Trench, RC. *Notes on the Parables of Our Lord*. Grand Rapids: Zondervan Publishing House, 1990.

Vitz, Paul. *Psychology as Religion: The Cult of Self-Worship*. Grand Rapids, William B. Eerdmans, 1977.

Wagner, Maurice. *The Sensation of Being Somebody*. Grand Rapids: Zondervan Publishing House, 1975.

Wallace, Ronald. *Calvin's Doctrine of the Christian Life*. Grand Rapids, William B. Eerdmans, n.d.

Walvoord, John F. *Jesus Christ Our Lord*. Chicago: Moody Press, 1969.

Watson, Thomas. *The Beatitudes*. Carlisle: Banner of Truth, 1968.

Wesley, John. *The Works of John Wesley*. Grand Rapids: Zondervan Publishing House, 1968.

About the Author

David M. Tyler, Ph.D. is the Director of Gateway Biblical Counseling and Training Center in Fairview Heights, Illinois. Dr. Tyler is the Dean of the Biblical Counseling Department of Master's International School of Divinity in Evansville, Indiana. He is an adjunct instructor at Calvary Bible College and Theological Seminary in Kansas City, Missouri. He is also the President of the American Academy of Biblical Counselors.

Dr. Tyler has authored numerous articles in professional periodicals, and the following books and booklets:

Books

Deceptive Diagnosis: When Sin is Called Sickness
(Co-authored)
ADHD: Deceptive Diagnosis (Co-authored)
God's Funeral: Psychology, Trading the Sacred for the Secular
The Second Coming of Jesus Christ: Oil,
Terrorism and Nuclear War
Jesus Christ: Self-Denial or Self-Esteem?
The Ape of God: How Satan, through the
Spiritual Formation Movement, Mimics God

Booklets

Self-Esteem: Are We Really Better Than We Think?
Grief: Victory over a Lonely Darkness

www.focuspublishing.com
www.davidmtyler.org